Discovering the New Testament

Discovering the New Testament

Simon Jones

Crossway Books

Leicester

CROSSWAY BOOKS
38 De Montfort Street, Leicester LE1 7GP, England
Website: www.ivpbooks.com
Email: ivp@uccf.org.uk

Discovering the New Testament is a revised and expanded edition of *A Rough Guide to the New Testament* (IVP, 1994). This edition first published 2001.

British Library Cataloguing in Publication Data
A catalogue record for this book is available from the British Library.

ISBN 1-85684-204-5

Set in Palatino
Typeset in Great Britain
Printed in Great Britain by Omnia Books Ltd, Glasgow

For
Donald Guthrie,
Steve Motyer, Dick France, Bob Willoughby
and Conrad Gempf,
who taught me and showed me by their lives
the truth of the New Testament.
Thanks, guys.

CONTENTS

Start here

The essential user's guide to this book

When was the last time you read the New Testament? I mean really read it. Not a handful of verses as part of a quiet time or daily devotion, not a short reading in church ahead of a sermon, but a great big dollop of a letter or a Gospel?

Indeed, have you *ever* read the New Testament as it was intended to be read before the versifiers and daily-reading guides got hold of it?

When Paul wrote to the church in Rome or Corinth he didn't send his letters in weekly ten-verse instalments. They arrived all at once, and were read out loud so that the church could hear the whole thing in one sitting. No doubt, having heard it once, people asked to hear various parts again, and then pored over and argued about what Paul meant by a particular phrase or word. But their first encounter was with the whole letter.

My hope is that this book will encourage you to do the same: to take a New Testament text – a Gospel, Acts or a letter – and read it at one sitting without pausing to think how a particular verse or word affects your life. Read these books as gripping stories from the frontline of the Christian faith. Allow yourself to get caught up in the whole sweep of an argument or immersed in the ebb and flow of a great epic.

Meeting the main man

The New Testament is about Jesus. Christians read it because they believe that in its pages they encounter him, learn what he taught and hear his voice speaking to them.

But Jesus lived two thousand years ago in a world very different from ours. There were no cars, TVs, mobile phones, fridges, microwaves or personal computers. People spoke long-dead languages, wore strange clothes and engaged in even stranger rituals at the meal table.

The action of the New Testament takes place in that world. So, not surprisingly, we find some of what it says puzzling, even off-putting; and that's why we don't read whole books at one sitting. We encounter an unfamiliar idea or activity and either rush off in search of a guide-book or sheepishly skip over the difficult bits.

The New Testament was written to explain Jesus to the first-century world, not to the twenty-first-century one. They didn't feel the need to explain the customs or ideas that we find puzzling, precisely because they didn't find them puzzling at all.

The apostles and others who penned the twenty-seven books that make up the New Testament had two things on their minds as they wrote. The first was purely domestic. The new movement had problems. The churches, filled with sinners who had been saved through faith in Jesus, weren't perfect. Troubles brewed, fights broke out, questions arose about which foods were acceptable and what people should wear to church. The apostles wrote to teach Christians about these and other matters.

The second purpose was to help the church to tell the world it lived in who Jesus was and what he had achieved through his life, death and resurrection in obscure little Palestine in the first decades of the first century.

After the apostles had written, the church gathered together the writings that were felt to be inspired and vital for building future generations of Christians. This collection forms what we now call the New Testament.

Your starter for ten

Because of the way the New Testament was written, readers today often have questions about it that are less to do with what it means and more to do with why its writers wrote it the way they did. For instance, why are there four accounts of Jesus' life (the four Gospels), three of which are very similar and one of which is very different? Why did Paul write letters and not short, helpful manuals on Christian living and running churches? How are we to make sense of Revelation?

And perhaps we're intrigued to know who the people were who wrote the New Testament – especially Paul, Luke and John, who penned so much of it. Where and how did they live, and why did they write?

The point of reading the New Testament is to meet Jesus. Doing a bit of background work helps us to set Jesus and the early Christians firmly and correctly in their context so that we can hear and see them more clearly. We need to do things in the right order, or what should be a background help risks becoming an alternative to encountering the story at first hand.

Charting a course

This book is in two distinct sections. The first twelve chapters enable you to work your way through the New Testament, on your own or with others, in such a way that you should end up with a good grasp of what each New Testament book is about, why it was written and how to hear God speaking to you through it about you and your situation.

The way to get the best out of this book, therefore, is to read the relevant chapter *before* you read the New Testament book or books the chapter talks about. You could start anywhere in the New Testament, though working through from the beginning is as good a way as any. So read chapter 1 and then read the synoptic Gospels. Or, if you really don't have time to do that, read the sections indicated at the beginning of the chapter.

It is always good to read the New Testament with others. Different readers see things differently and bring a variety of insights to bear on the text. If you are reading this book as a group, two things will enhance your experience of the New Testament. The first is that it's good to read whole books together out loud, to hear the text as those for whom it was written would have heard it. If you don't want to read it, there are plenty of tapes available for you to listen to. (This is a good way to encounter the New Testament on your own as well.) Secondly, it's best to make sure that every group member has a copy of this book so that they can read the relevant chapter and any background notes the chapter refers to.

The second section – chapters 13–23 – aims to give you the essential background to the world of the New Testament in bite-sized chunks: how people thought, what they believed if they didn't believe in Jesus, how the church grew and spread from Palestine to Rome and beyond, and what it was like to go to church in the first century.

The first section refers you to the second section from time to time, to fill in background necessary for a better understanding of the particular New Testament book you're reading. If you want to get the best out of this book, it's a good idea to read the chapter or pages referred to in a particular study at that point; they will help you grasp what a particular New Testament author is saying and why he's saying it that way. The studies will also refer you other books in the Crossway Bible Guide series which give much more detail on the book you're studying.

Getting ready

So, read the relevant chapter in this book. Then read the New Testament text or texts under review. Then talk about it with your friends. My prayer is that by doing that you'll meet Jesus in a new and life-changing way. And that, after all, is the whole point of reading the New Testament.

PART ONE

Twelve steps to discovering the New Testament

Put that in triplicate

Matthew, Mark and Luke

We're at the start of an awfully big adventure. We're about to encounter the most fascinating, charismatic man ever to grace the planet. Hold on to your hats because over the next week we'll read this chapter and the synoptic Gospels. You can either follow the plan below or read all the Gospels being studied right through each day on days 2–5. (This is a tall order for the Synoptics, though you could read Mark, Matthew and Luke over three days and then return to bits that caught your attention on the fourth). However you do it, prepare for a life-changing encounter.

Day 1 Read this chapter.
Day 2 Read Mark 1 – 16.
Day 3 Read Matthew 1 – 13; Luke 1:1 – 9:50.
Day 4 Read Matthew 14 – 20; Luke 9:51 – 19:27.
Day 5 Read Matthew 21 – 26; Luke 19:28 – 24:53.
Day 6 Re-read this chapter and look at the discussion questions.
Day 7 Meet with the friends you are reading this book with, have a meal or a drink, and talk through the discussion questions and anything else that struck you through your reading.

'So tell me who this Jesus was, then.' The man holding a samosa in one hand and a pint in the other was serious. He knew nothing about Jesus. And why should he? After all, Jesus lived in Israel in the first century, he lives in Camberwell in the twenty-first, and no-one has ever introduced them.

As the church grew and spread around the Roman Empire, Christians met more and more people who said, 'So tell me who this Jesus was, then.' And so they passed on the stories about Jesus they had been told, or they recalled the events they themselves had witnessed.

Someone might have recalled the miraculous catch of fish as an example that Jesus had authority over nature (Luke 5:1–11). Someone else might have remembered the way Jesus touched lepers and healed them, showing his love and power (Luke 5:12–16). Another might have described the fiery way Jesus had spoken about the religious leaders of his day (Luke 11:37–53).

Soon after the church had exploded on to an unsuspecting world, some people began to collect these stories about Jesus – stories that showed people what he was like, what and how he taught, and why we should follow him. No doubt, as the Christians gathered for worship every week, various stories about Jesus would be told. It is almost certain that every week the story of Jesus' death and resurrection would be told and remembered as the Christians shared bread and wine together.

Eventually – probably as early as the 40s and 50s (Jesus died probably in AD 33) – these stories began to be gathered together and edited into collections and books. Our New Testament opens with four of these collections or Gospels. Three of them, Matthew, Mark and Luke, are very similar. They are known as the synoptic Gospels, and they are the subject of this chapter.

At the beginning of his Gospel, Luke explains his reason for writing:

Since many have undertaken to set down an orderly account of the events that have been fulfilled among us, just as they were handed on to us by those who from the beginning were eyewitnesses and servants of the word, I too decided, after investigating everything carefully from the very first, to write an orderly account for you, most excellent Theophilus, so that you may know the truth concerning the things about which you have been instructed (Luke 1:1–4).

'The facts, Lewis, give me the facts'

Lots of people had put pen to parchment by the time Luke started. But Luke, who had not known Jesus in the flesh, wanted to check out the facts for himself. He also wanted to provide an accurate picture of Jesus for Theophilus, possibly a wealthy recent convert who was footing the bill for Luke's enterprise. He was a bit like Lewis filling Inspector Morse in at the beginning of a case: woe betide him if he didn't get his facts straight!

So Luke set about 'investigating everything carefully'. It is possible that he was able to do this during the two-year period in the late 50s in which Paul, with whom Luke frequently travelled and for whom he may have acted as a secretary, was in prison in Caesarea.

During that time Luke could well have travelled south into Galilee, where Jesus had lived most of his life. There Luke would have talked to people about Jesus. It is entirely possible that he talked to Jesus' family, maybe even to Mary, about the events surrounding Jesus' birth – for only Luke records them.

It is also quite likely that he had a copy of Mark's Gospel, or, at least, a version of something very like Mark's Gospel which provided the order in which the key events of Jesus' life and ministry happened. Both Luke and Matthew follow Mark's order of events quite closely. So it is most likely (because Mark is the shortest of the three Synoptics) that he wrote first and the other two used his account (or a version of it) as the skeleton which they fleshed out with their fuller versions of the story of Jesus. The tradition that Peter was Mark's source for his work is entirely plausible. The two men travelled together and settled for some considerable time in Rome, where Mark could have set down Peter's recollection of Jesus' life and teaching (see chapter 10).

But Luke's Gospel, like the other two, is more than just a list of events, an account of what happened in Jesus' life. It was written with a very definite purpose: to explain who Jesus was, the significance of his coming and especially the meaning of his death and resurrection.

The Gospels are not biographies of Jesus, like the ones we might read about a rock legend or movie star, a politician or a missionary pioneer. Modern biographies give exhaustive (and often exhausting!) details of their subject's home life and schooling, pastimes and hobbies, love-life and contribution to history.

No-one wrote that sort of biography in the ancient world. Ancient writers were not much interested in personal details about their subjects – their psychology, their family relationships, their favourite foods. They were much more interested in their exploits. So the biographies of the Roman emperors were full of accounts of battles and treaties, and showed their subjects as models of virtuous behaviour.

Well, the Gospels are a bit like that. They concentrate on telling us what Jesus did and said. They show us clearly that he lived a good and God-honouring life. But they go further than that.

'Walk this way, please ...'

The Gospels' prime purpose is to show us why we should put our faith in Jesus as the Son of God and the Saviour of the world, the one through whom God's new world order came bursting into life. The authors are not writing light entertainment, stirring tales or even a moving account of a great religious leader. They are calling readers to put their faith in Jesus, to follow him, to live the way he lived and to become part of the family he founded: that is, the church. This was especially important as the church grew among the Gentiles. Why should they put their trust in a Jewish rabbi? What did his story have to say to them about their lives, their hopes, their relationship with God?

Mark begins his account like this: 'The beginning of the

good news [or gospel] of Jesus Christ, the Son of God' (Mark 1:1). Before the word 'gospel' meant a type of book, it meant the proclamation of what God had done and was doing through Jesus. As Paul says, 'The gospel ... is the power of God for salvation to everyone who has faith' (Romans 1:16).

This does not mean that the Gospels are fairy stories or works of fiction or fantasy. That's why Luke stresses to Theophilus that he has carefully investigated what happened, he has talked to eyewitnesses, he has weighed one story with another and has distilled the results of all his enquiries into an account that he believes is accurate and true. And, of course, we now believe that the Holy Spirit was helping him with his enquiries.

Finding our way through the story

Luke, Matthew and Mark offer us an outline of Jesus' life and ministry that stresses why we should believe that he is the Son of God and the Saviour of the world. John's Gospel has the same purpose but is written in a different style (more on this in the next chapter).

The basic outline of the gospel story is this. John the Baptist appeared urging the people of Israel to get ready because God was coming in fulfilment of his promises made long ago through the prophets. Then Jesus appeared and was baptized by John in the Jordan, thus throwing in his lot with the reform movement John headed up. After John was arrested for criticizing Herod's marital arrangements, Jesus carried on a ministry of teaching, healing and exorcism in Galilee. He gained something of a reputation and a following. The ordinary folk loved what he said because he made them feel as though they mattered to God. The religious leaders, the Pharisees and scribes (see chapter 15), were suspicious of him at first, and then openly hostile. They regarded him as a threat not only to their position in society but also to the faith of Israel which they saw it as their duty to protect. Jesus' version of what God was up to was diametrically opposed to theirs. The conflict was bound to end in tears. After about three years Jesus went up to Jerusalem for the Passover, was arrested (following an incident in the temple, where he had attempted to throw out the money-changers and animal-sellers) and was crucified. On the third day he rose from the dead and appeared to his disciples.

Within this basic outline, the synoptic writers tell stories about Jesus' teaching and exploits that confirm their claim that he was the Son of God. All of them tell of the time when Jesus fed five thousand people with a little boy's packed lunch, of the time when he calmed a fierce storm that blew up on the Sea of Galilee, and of the time when he rode into Jerusalem on a donkey, in conscious fulfilment of Old Testament prophecy about a coming king.

All the Gospels picture Jesus telling great stories with punchlines that made the listeners either hoot with laughter or else wince with recognition that the sinner or hypocrite or the foolish girl was actually them. We call these stories 'parables', and even two thousand years later they have not lost their power to make us think, repent and return to God with renewed faith and gratitude.

To this basic outline Matthew and Luke add details and stories not found in Mark. For instance, both give an account of Jesus' birth, stressing, through different aspects of the event, that he was born in fulfilment of the promises of God contained in the Old Testament (Matthew 1 – 2; Luke 1 – 2). All the Gospel-writers, in fact, are keen to show that there is a strong link between the history of Israel and the ministry of Jesus.

Matthew seems to have had a great interest in Jesus as a teacher, and gathers large quantities of his teaching into various sections of his Gospel. The most famous is the Sermon on the Mount, which is found in chapters 5 – 7. But there's also a collection of parables in chapter 13, a section of teaching on relationships between disciples in chapter 18 and a large chunk of material on the future in chapters 23 and 24.

Luke, by contrast, had a keen sense of what makes a gripping story. He composed his Gospel in such a way as to heighten the drama, especially the sense of growing conflict between Jesus, the Galilean rabbi and the Jewish authorities, whose centre of power was in Jerusalem. The middle section of his Gospel, 9:51 – 19:27, which contains many stories not found in any other Gospel, describes Jesus' journey from the northern territory of Galilee (where he had a reputation and was even something of a hero) south to Jerusalem, the capital, the place where his opponents called the shots. As this journey – known by scholars as 'the travel narrative' for obvious reasons – brings him closer and closer to Jerusalem, the tension is electrifying.

Getting to the heart of the story

All the Gospels devote a large amount of space to the last week of Jesus' life. The last five and a half chapters of Luke, the last six chapters of Mark and the last eight chapters of Matthew are devoted to Jesus' last week and its aftermath. So great is the stress on these final seven days that some people have suggested that the Gospels are really passion narratives (stories of Jesus' death and resurrection) with brief scene-setting introductions.

This is an exaggeration, of course. But each Gospel focuses on Jesus' final week with an intensity not focused on any other event in his life. The reason for this is simple: the death and resurrection of Jesus lie at the very heart of the good news that Christians want to proclaim to the world.

So the Gospel-writers spell out in detail what happened. They start with the entry of Jesus into Jerusalem at the head of a column of excited pilgrims from Galilee who are up for the feast and full of expectation that the kingdom of God is about to dawn, with Jesus, the prophet, as its instigator and head. Once in the city, Jesus' first call is the temple, where he makes a whip and drives out the money-changers and animal-sellers, accusing them and the ruling authorities – the priests and the Sadducees – of turning a house of prayer for all nations into a den of robbers. This demonstration, during which Jesus is very clearly claiming to be greater than the temple – indeed, to be replacing it as the focus of

God's activity in the world – leads directly to his arrest.

Before the ruling authorities make their move, they get one of the Twelve (Judas) to agree to betray him. Then there is the quiet interlude of a last meal with his close group of disciples (the Twelve), Jesus' anguished prayer in the Garden of Gethsemane, his arrest, Peter's denial, Jesus' trial before the Jewish Sanhedrin (the high priest and council of elders), his trial before Pilate, and his crucifixion. Each Gospel tackles it slightly differently, and Luke adds that Jesus was also seen by Herod, king of Galilee (Luke 23:6–12). But the basic outline is the same in all three synoptic Gospels.

It's clear that these facts mattered to the early Christians. The reason for this is not difficult to see: Jesus' death and resurrection were the basis of their proclamation of salvation in his name. His death opened the way for God to forgive anyone who put their trust in his sacrifice for them on the cross. His death was the victory of God over the powers that oppress all people, not just in Israel but in the pagan world as well. In Jesus' death, the creator God was restating his claim to the allegiance of all the peoples of every nation on the earth. Thus, while the letters, especially those of Paul, spell out what the death of Jesus means, the Gospel-writers carefully and accurately tell us what actually took place on that fearful yet glorious Friday.

And each of them places the record of the final meal which Jesus had with his friends right at the centre of their narrative of these events. They probably did this for two reasons. First, it explains where the practice of Christians meeting together and sharing bread and wine originated. Matthew, Mark and Luke – along with Paul – preserve the words that Jesus spoke at the first Lord's Supper, words that have been used ever since, everywhere in the world where Christians break bread together (Matthew 26:26–30; Mark 14:12–26; Luke 22:7–38; 1 Corinthians 11:23–26).

Secondly, it is the synoptic writers' way of telling us what the events of Good Friday, which they are about to set out for us in detail, actually mean. This is not just the story of a popular teacher who fell foul of the powers that be, was accused of falsely claiming Israel's throne and the people's allegiance, and was condemned and executed – though it is, of course, all those things. It is also the story of how Jesus offered himself for the sins of the world, how in his broken body and shed blood God was making a new agreement between himself and his people (represented in one single suffering individual), and through them the whole world (see chapter 3 on Acts).

So, whereas ancient biographies concentrated on how the lives of their subjects were exemplary, the Gospels focus on how the death of Jesus fulfils the prophecies about him and achieves God's purpose of putting people right with himself and offering them new life.

But, of course, the Gospels don't end with Jesus in the grave. A dead Messiah, for all his grand words about giving himself for others, would be no Messiah at all.

Each Gospel climaxes with an empty tomb and a risen Jesus who showed himself to his followers on numerous occasions and in various places. Jesus is alive, they declare. What human beings did on Good Friday, God reversed on Easter Day. While Mark almost certainly left it there (his Gospel originally ending at 16:8), Matthew and Luke go on to tell us that the risen Jesus commanded his followers to go and tell the world the news of his death and resurrection, the news of forgiveness and new life (Matthew 28; Luke 24).

Are you sitting comfortably?

The Gospels seem to have been written primarily to teach newly converted Christians about the founder of their faith. The material is presented in bite-sized chunks, each containing an insight into Jesus' life and character or a slice of his teaching on how to live as his disciples in the world.

It seems that from a very early stage – almost certainly before AD 100 – the synoptic Gospels were being used in the weekly worship of the church. They offered every Christian believer access to the earthly life of Jesus. Then, as now, they inspired, challenged and nourished the faith of ordinary men and women who, in their daily lives, were seeking to live as he lived.

So the man with the samosa who says, 'Tell me who this Jesus was, then', needs to hear the stories Matthew, Mark and Luke told in the lively, honest way they told them.

Questions

1. Although Matthew, Mark and Luke wrote basically the same story, they wrote for slightly different reasons. What is distinctive about each writer's portrait of Jesus? (You might find it useful to use a study Bible and the individual CBG volumes on the Synoptics to help you with this.)

   Read Matthew 9:18–26; Mark 5:21–43; and Luke 8:40–56.
   (a) What are the differences between the ways in which the writers tell these stories?
   (b) What do we learn from the stories?

2. Look at the accounts of the last Supper in Matthew (26:17–30), Mark (14:12–26) and Luke (22:7–38). What are the differences between these accounts and what are the similarities? What key point do you think each writer is trying to make in his account? How does having three accounts of the same event enrich our appreciation of what actually happened?

3. Matthew's Sermon on the Mount (Matthew 5 – 7) and Luke's Sermon on the Plain (Luke 6:17–49) lay out Jesus' manifesto of discipleship. What do you make of the difference of emphasis between the two accounts? Does it give you a fuller picture of Jesus' manifesto or leave you wondering which writer is closer to the truth?

Now make it a quartet

John's Gospel

Having got caught up in the adventure of Jesus' life and ministry, we're now ready for an even closer encounter with the man himself. This week's challenge is to read this chapter and John's Gospel. On days 2–5 you could read the whole Gospel each day. By the end of the week you'd have a heck of a grasp of its central message – not to mention having drunk deeply at the feet of the Master. Alternatively, follow the plan.

Day 1 Read this chapter.
Day 2 Read John 1 – 5.
Day 3 Read John 6 – 11.
Day 4 Read John 12 – 17.
Day 5 Read John 18 – 21.
Day 6 Re-read this chapter and look at the discussion questions.
Day 7 Meet with the friends you are reading this book with, have a meal or a drink, and talk through the discussion questions and anything else that struck you through your reading.

In some ways the synoptic Gospels are like a tune tapped out with a single finger of the right hand. They give us a line-sketch of Jesus. It is very interesting, even compelling; but much of the depths in Jesus' character and personality are only hinted at and not really filled out in detail. We find ourselves asking for more.

Then we get to John. John is to the Synoptics what the left hand and chords are to the simple one-finger piano tune. John fills out the synoptic portrait of Jesus by adding depth and breadth to the picture. John's Gospel was probably the last to be written, though the stories that are unique to it probably circulated from the earliest days of the church. It is probably also the only Gospel to have been written by one of the twelve disciples of Jesus. It has all the hallmarks of being the account of an eyewitness. It is full of little details that suggest the author saw and heard, felt and took part in the stories he is telling.

Those who stress how different John is from the Synoptics often do so by focusing on the details. When you look at the broad picture, however, what you notice is how similar John is to the Synoptics. The outline of Jesus' ministry from John the Baptist to the crucifixion is broadly the same. The picture of Jesus that emerges, though nuanced differently, still emphasizes his role as a prophet, teacher and healer, and still has characters in the story raise the question of whether he might or might not be the longed-for Messiah. The crowds in John respond more favourably to Jesus than the religious leaders do – just as in the Synoptics.

Furthermore, if you compare the Synoptics, John and the host of apocryphal Gospels that circulated in the first and second centuries, including the *Gospel of Thomas* (which is widely agreed to contain authentic stories and sayings of Jesus that aren't in any of the canonical Gospels), what strikes you is how similar the four are to each other and how different from any of the non-canonical Gospels.

'Tell us another, Grandpa'

Tradition has it that John wrote his Gospel in Ephesus when he was an old man. It was as if all the other Gospels had come out and had topped the Christian best-seller lists, and John's friends were saying to him, 'Come on, you tell 'em what you know.' Eventually, after much persuading, he took up his pen or dictated his memories and stories to a secretary.

John probably knew of the synoptic Gospels. He knew what was in them. He knew who they were written for. He did not want to produce yet another book that said the same things to a similar audience.

Mark and Luke wrote in answer to questions from mainly Gentile converts about the founder of Christianity; they wanted to know what Jesus was like. John, like Matthew, appears to have written with mainly Jewish Christians in mind.

The situation was probably something like this. In the final quarter of the first century, after the Romans had destroyed Jerusalem in AD 70, the scattered Jews struggled to keep their faith and traditions alive. At the same time, the Christian church was staking its claim to be a religion separate from both the Judaism it had sprung from and the paganism it encountered in every city of the Empire.

Jewish Christians – people who had been born Jews but who had come to believe that Jesus was the Messiah promised by the Old Testament – felt squeezed. On the one hand, Gentile Christians were not adopting many of the practices Jewish Christians thought were important: circumcision, the Old Testament dietary laws, and keeping the Sabbath. On the other hand, the leaders of Judaism were stressing that you could not be loyal to your Jewish roots and accept the claims made by Christians about Jesus of Nazareth.

Many of these Jewish Christians were in danger of losing their faith. Until John wrote his Gospel. What they needed to hear was not the basic story of who Jesus was, what he did, how he died and that he rose gain. They knew all that from other sources. What they needed was a fresh angle on Jesus' story that would answer their specific needs.

It's the way you tell 'em

Two visitors to Britain, who know nothing of the country's

life, politics or culture, decide to find out what's going on by buying a national daily newspaper. One buys *The Mirror*, the other *The Independent*. Were they to compare notes, they would probably wonder if they had been reading about the same country.

Of course, there is overlap between the content of *The Mirror* and *The Independent*. Where they cover the same story, they usually agree on the basic outline of the facts. That they are very different papers – in tone, content and layout – is due to the fact that they are written for very different audiences. The questions an *Independent* reader is asking are very different from those posed by a reader of *The Mirror*.

Perhaps this helps us to get the differences between John and the Synoptics in proportion. Where all four Gospels write about the same event, they pretty much agree on the basic outline. What they differ on is the level of information provided. John goes into far more detail. This can be seen by comparing the accounts in all four Gospels of, for example, the feeding of the five thousand and the trial of Jesus (John 6:1–15; Matthew 14:13–21; John 18:12 – 19:16; Matthew 26:57 – 27:31).

John leaves out many things that Matthew, Mark and Luke tell us about. He is silent about the birth and baptism of Jesus, the calling of the Twelve, the exorcisms, the parables, the transfiguration and the institution of the Lord's Supper. But, as we have already noted, he probably didn't feel compelled to include any of these because three other books in circulation already told believers about them.

And as he himself says, there are 'many other things that Jesus did; if every one of them were written down, I suppose that the world itself could not contain the books that would be written' (John 21:25). In other words, he has to be selective and there's no point going over old ground, especially when he has so many wonderful stories that the others left out of their accounts: the turning of water into wine (2:1–11), Jesus' early ministry in Judea (2:13 – 3:36), his trip to Samaria and meeting with the Samaritan woman (4:1–42), the healing of the man at the pool of Bethzatha

(5:1–29), the raising of Lazarus (11:1–44) and his frequent visits to Jerusalem (e.g. 7:10–52).

Speaking from experience

Another way to illustrate the relationship is to see them as histories of the same events written by insiders and outsiders. The historian Ben Pimlot produced a huge, detailed and magisterial account of the Wilson years. No stone is left unturned, no document unexamined, no participant in or observer of those days uninterviewed. But Pimlot was not a member of that government. In that respect he is like Luke. Tony Benn, by contrast, produced a series of volumes of his diaries, written while he was a member of Wilson's Cabinet, a participant in events and decisions. In that respect he is like John.

John was an eyewitness. The author of the Gospel was the son of Zebedee, the brother of James, Jesus' best friend on earth, the only one of the inner circle to put pen to paper. This, no doubt, made him much more confident about his material. Matthew, Mark and Luke did not include anything in their Gospels that they aren't absolutely sure of, that they couldn't actually check out. Hence the short speeches of Jesus, the easily remembered, one-sentence sayings, the briefly told incidents.

John, on the other hand, heard Jesus' teaching for three solid years. He heard the same things often, and probably talked them over – indeed, argued about them late into the night with Jesus and the other disciples. The words of Jesus soaked into him and became a part of the way he thought and hence remembered. So when he wrote his memoirs of Jesus' life, he was able to recall long speeches Jesus had made, and to comment on their meaning for their original audience and for John's current readers. (An example is 3:1–36. Look at where various versions and commentators think the direct speech of Jesus ends and John's comments take over. What do you think?) He remembered the minute details of incidents that he had witnessed, even the tone of voice adopted by Jesus' opponents.

Scratching where people itch

But that doesn't account for all the differences between John and the other Gospels. Why are there so few incidents in John's account? Why are there no synoptic-style parables? Why is the cleansing of the temple at the start and not at the end of Jesus' ministry?

We need to remind ourselves who John was writing for. His Gospel was for Jewish Christians who were under pressure to abandon their new-found faith in Christ and return to traditional Judaism. John wanted to show them clearly why such a course of action would be disastrous.

The way he did this was to recount what Jesus did and said about the major festivals and institutions of the Jewish people and about the key figures from Israel's past who helped to define what a true Jew was. John wanted to show that it was Jesus who was now the focus of God's activity in the world, and no longer the temple and feasts of the Jewish calendar.

This probably explains why the cleansing of the temple comes at the beginning of John's Gospel, whereas according to Matthew, Mark and Luke it happened in the last week of Jesus' life. John could well have placed that story at the start of his account of Jesus' ministry as a kind of summary statement (John 2:13–22).

What he is saying is this. The Jesus you will meet in this Gospel is such an important figure in God's purposes for Israel and the world that he is replacing the temple. The temple stood at the heart of Jewish faith and practice (see chapters 12 and 13): it was where Jewish people, and Gentiles who were attracted to the Jewish way of life, could go to pray and especially to find forgiveness for sins through the offering of animal sacrifices. This is probably why John tells us that John the Baptist described Jesus as 'the Lamb of God who takes away the sin of the world' (1:29–34). In a world where the temple had been destroyed, John was reminding Jewish Christians that it was Jesus, not a building in Jerusalem, that was the focus of forgiveness and God's presence in the world.

John uniquely shows us that Jesus often went up to Jerusalem to take part in the major festivals. For example, chapters 7 and 8 are set during the Feast of Tabernacles. This is traditionally when the people lived in tents on their roofs as a way of recalling the Israelites' journey through the wilderness after the exodus. It was also a festival that looked forward to the day when God would send his Holy Spirit and establish his rule on earth.

This looking back and looking forward found its focus in a ceremony that happened every day of the seven days of the feast. The priests would draw water from the pool of Siloam, parade through the streets of Jerusalem with it and pour it over the altar in the temple. The water would stream out from the temple through the city, a visual aid reminding the people of how God had provided water in the desert and of how Ezekiel had seen a vision of living water streaming from the temple when the kingdom of God had come in all its splendour and fullness (Ezekiel 47:1–12).

It was on the last and greatest day of the feast, when the water ceremony had happened for the seventh time, that Jesus said: 'Let anyone who is thirsty come to me and let the one who believes in me drink.' In this dramatic story John shows that Jesus was claiming to fulfil all the expectations of the Feast of Tabernacles. He was the one who would bring in the kingdom of God. He was the one who would pour out the Holy Spirit on his people (John 7:37–39).

'Give us a sign'

To reinforce this key claim that Jesus is the focus of God's saving activity on earth, John has composed his account by putting together several 'signs' – he doesn't call them miracles – surrounded by stories that throw light on what the signs tell us about Jesus.

They are: turning water into wine (2:1–11); healing the nobleman's son at Capernaum (4:46–54); healing the man at the pool (5:1–9); feeding the five thousand (6:1–15); walking on water (6:16–21); healing the blind man (9:1–8); raising Lazarus from death (11:1–44); Jesus' resurrection (20:1–29) and the miraculous catch of fish (21:1–14). The meaning of each of these signs is then explained by Jesus or John (with the possible exception of the changing of water into wine), with the focus being on what the signs tell us about Jesus.

What about our heroes?

John also uses some key stories and personalities from Israel's history to show that in Jesus' life, death and resurrection that history is reaching its climax and all the promises of the past are being fulfilled. So, for instance, there is the debate between Jesus and the Pharisees about who are the true children of Abraham (8:31–59). The key issue here is: 'Who are the true people of God: those allied to Jesus or those loyal to the emerging rabbinical Judaism?' In the sometimes acrimonious atmosphere of the late first century, it was important for Jewish believers to remember that through faith in Jesus they were the true descendants of Abraham.

Moses is first introduced in the magnificent prologue to the Gospel (see below). But he crops up all through John's narrative (1:45; 3:14; 5:45–46; 6:32; 7:19, 22–23; 9:28–29) where the stories about the giving of the law, the wilderness wanderings and the true meaning of what Moses said lie behind John's story about Jesus and his disputes with the religious establishment of his day. And again, the key issue is: 'Who are the true people of God?' And the key lesson for John's first readers was: 'Listen to Jesus, not the rabbis, who tell you that their way is the true way.'

Then John portrays Jesus as the true shepherd foreseen by Ezekiel (Ezekiel 34), the one who would be the prophet like Moses, only greater; the king like David, only greater; the Lord himself come to lead his people (as foreshadowed in Isaiah 40 – 55; see 6:25–71; 10:11–18; 19:31–36).

All this is wrapped up in two ringing declarations about who Jesus is. The first is 1:1–18, where John recalls the creation of the world by God's Word and then tells us that that Word became flesh and lived with us. The second is Thomas's statement about Jesus a week after the resurrection: 'My Lord and my God' (John 20:28). Here again John is reminding Jewish Christians – fierce monotheists of long standing – that the focus of God's activity in the world has shifted from the temple (which has been destroyed) and the law (which is becoming associated with the growing power of the rabbis) to Jesus – God's word made flesh, as much of God as can be contained in a human frame. Such bold claims were vital if the fragile faith of these Jewish Christians was to be strengthened.

The prologue to the Gospel is a magnificent introduction of John's major themes, especially the theme of God's love for the whole world and his intention through Jesus to fulfil his promise to Abraham that through his descendants the whole earth would be blessed and enjoy the benefits of knowing their creator personally. You can see this clearly in parallelism of 1:10–11. Verse 11 speaks of Jesus coming to Israel but being rejected by them. Verse 10 speaks of him coming to the world but the world not knowing him. At the end of the Gospel, the disciples are sent by Jesus into the world to remedy that situation (20:21–23; see also 12:20–24, 32; 17:18–23).

In the prologue there are clear echoes of Genesis 1, the great Jewish story of how God created the heavens and the earth. But there is also an echo of a poem that many of John's readers would have been very familiar with. It comes from chapter 24 of Ecclesiasticus (a book in our Apocrypha that is more properly called The Wisdom of Jesus ben Sirach). It was written a century or so before the birth of Christ to demonstrate that the wisdom that comes from following Yahweh, the God of Israel, is greater than that of any pagan philosopher. It lauded God's wisdom and personified her as active in the creation of the world, an extension of the personality of God himself. For Sirach, the true way of being Israel was to follow this wisdom embodied in what God revealed of himself to Moses on Sinai, that is, the law. John takes this and applies it not to Moses but to Jesus (see the contrast in 1:17). If you want to know the wisdom that was active in the creation of the world, says John, look at Jesus and nowhere else (1:18).

Keep the faith

John is a pastor. He loves the people God has put in his care. He wants to strengthen their faith and encourage them to stay loyal to its founder. And so he has written a Gospel that warmly and compassionately shows us that Jesus is in fact God in the flesh, the one through whom we receive life and hope, grace and peace, the kingdom of God and the Holy Spirit.

As he himself says about the purpose of his writing, 'these things are written so that you might continue to believe that Jesus is the Messiah, the Son of God, and believing you may have life in his name' (20:31).

Questions

1. Read John 6. (It's a long chapter but well worth the effort). It is John's account of the feeding of the five thousand (see Matthew 14:13–21; Mark 6:32–44; Luke 9:10–17) and Jesus walking on the water (see Matthew 14:22–33; Mark 6:47–51). Ask yourself these three questions:
   (a) What do we learn about this incident from John that we don't learn from the Synoptics?
   (b) What do we learn about Jesus from John's account that we don't learn from Matthew, Mark and Luke?
   (c) Why do you think John told it the way he did?
2. The prologue of John's Gospel wonderfully pictures Jesus as the 'Word of God', taking ideas from Jewish wisdom and applying them to the central figure of our faith. Can you construct a similarly powerful picture of Jesus out of contemporary religious ideas such as teaching that comes from the New Age?
3. Look at the signs that John hangs his story on (see pages 31–32). What do they tell about who Jesus is and why he came?

3

What Jesus did next

The Acts of the Apostles

Much like the aerobics instructor upping your quota of bench presses, my aim for you this week is to read this chapter and the Acts of the Apostles. For the super-fit, days 2–5 could be filled reading the whole of Acts each day. You'll feel the burn but the pay-off will be terrific. Alternatively, follow the already challenging plan. New Testament fitness waits at the end of either course.

Day 1 Read this chapter.
Day 2 Read Acts 1 – 7.
Day 3 Read Acts 8 – 15.
Day 4 Read Acts 16 – 22:29.
Day 5 Read Acts 22:30 – 28:31.
Day 6 Re-read this chapter and look at the discussion questions.
Day 7 Meet with the friends you are reading this book with, have a meal or a drink, and talk through the discussion questions and anything else that struck you through your reading.

Atlanta burns, the future's up for grabs and Rhet Butler turns to Scarlett O'Hara and utters his immortal lines: 'Frankly, my dear, I don't give a damn.' The credits roll and the audience is left hanging.

Forty years later a publisher in America realized that a lot of people frankly did give a damn and wanted to know what happened to the hapless heroine of *Gone With the Wind*. So the publisher paid an author $1 million to write the sequel.

Luke's Gospel ends with Jesus going up into heaven and the believers skipping back to Jerusalem full of beans and new life. But what happened then? What became of Peter, James, John and the others? What became of Jesus and his message? Alone of the Gospel-writers, Luke sets out to tell us in his unique second volume known to us as the Acts of the Apostles. Perhaps it ought to have been called *What Jesus Did Next*.

Acts opens in Jerusalem and closes in Rome. On the way it visits a lot of large cities between those capitals and a few smaller ones too. It tells how churches were set up, how the good news of Jesus spread to people of all kinds, classes and backgrounds and what happened to some of the key players in the Gospels.

But as a sequel Acts is also a bit of a puzzle. Peter disappears half-way through and none of the other apostles except James, John's brother (executed in chapter 12), gets a look-in. From chapter 9 onwards, Paul dominates the book. But even his story is unfinished. The last scene in Acts is of Paul awaiting trial, and we cry out, 'What happened next?' As far as we know, Luke never wrote volume three.

The edited highlights

One of the cornerstones of TV sports coverage is the edited-highlights programme. This is where the broadcasters bring us not the whole game but just the exciting, important bits. If it's soccer, they show us the goals and the near-misses; if it's cricket, they show us the runs and wickets.

Well, Luke gives us the edited highlights of the history the church from around AD 30 to the early 60s. But in order to read Acts right, we need to get a handle on why he selected the highlights he did and not others. What was it about the stories he tells us that attracted his attention?

If we can identify the main point Luke was trying to

make in writing Acts, we'll be a long way down the road of grasping why he wrote it as he did. And the best way to do that is to find out who he was writing for. What questions were they asking? How does he answer them?

Some have said that he was writing to show the church at the tail end of the first century how the good news of Jesus spread from Jerusalem (a pretty obscure place) to every major city of the Empire, including Rome. After all, he begins with Jesus telling the Twelve to tell the world about him, starting in Judea, spreading out through Samaria and heading for the ends of the earth (1:8). And certainly the movement of people in Acts follows that pattern: starting in Jerusalem (2 – 6), moving out through Samaria (8), and north to Antioch (11:19–31), Turkey, Greece and Rome. But while this could well have been part of Luke's purpose, it doesn't account for the way his book is put together.

Others suggest he was writing to reassure the Roman authorities that the church was a peaceful religious movement and not a wild bunch of radicals hell-bent on overthrowing the state. After all, the founder of the church, Jesus of Nazareth, had been crucified by the Roman government of Judea for challenging its power. And Paul, whose journey to Rome dominates the end of the book, had gone there to stand trial. This could explain why the outcome of the trial is unknown: Luke rushed this volume out as evidence of Paul's honourable conduct.

Acts, like Luke's Gospel, is dedicated to the wealthy Gentile believer Theophilus. Perhaps he needed reassuring that he wasn't signing up to and funding a terrorist outfit. And it's true that the Roman authorities get a good press from Luke. The people who oppose the church and give the Christians a hard time in the courts are usually Jews (e.g. 13:50; 17:1–9) and sometimes people involved in other religions whose livelihood is threatened by the arrival of Christianity, such as the idol-makers in Ephesus (19:23–41).

But again, while Luke wanted to commend the good news of Jesus to the Roman authorities and to ensure that the church was not opposed for the wrong reasons, there's more to Acts than this.

Who can you trust these days?

Luke was clearly writing for an educated readership. His is a carefully constructed story, a work of history, not a hastily dashed-off pamphlet. This means he was more than likely writing for city-dwellers, which explains why most of the action of Acts takes place in cities. We hear virtually nothing of the church of Galilee, where the movement started, where Jesus lived and worked most of his life, and where the bulk of the action in the Gospels happened – though we know from other sources that the church existed there in the villages and fishing communities from the earliest days. James's letter may well have been written to Christians there as well as to those in Judea and Samaria.

Luke was also a friend of Paul. They travelled together, preached the good news together, ate together and no doubt talked long into the night about what their message meant to the world they lived in, especially how that message spoke to the great division in the world between Jew and Gentile. Paul was the Jew who had become an apostle to the Gentiles, and Luke was the Gentile who had thrown in his lot with an obscure Jewish sect; how did the good news of Jesus bring them together (16:11; Colossians 4:14)?

When Paul tackled the issue of this ethnic and cultural division, he did so in his typical robust style in the letter to the Galatians, and then later, in more measured tones, when writing to the church at Rome and Ephesus (see chapters 4 and 5). When Luke tackled it he did so in a story, just he had done with the life and teaching of Jesus. Luke's story of the growth and spread of the church was written to show that God can be trusted: he keeps his promises and he fulfils his plans. Specifically, Luke shows us that God kept his promise to Abraham to create one people for himself out of all the nations of the earth through the church's proclamation of Jesus around the world of the Roman Empire. At the start of his Gospel Luke records the song of praise that Mary sang after the angel had visited her. In that song she told the world that God had kept his promise to Abraham – the promise that the world would be saved through a child born to his family (Luke 1:46–55; Genesis 12). The gospel ends with Jesus, having suffered on the cross for the sins of the whole world, sending his followers out to invite the world to join them (Luke 24:45–49). For the promise to Abraham could not be fulfilled if all that Jesus achieved was to found a renewal movement within first-century Judaism. The message of Jesus had to break out of the straitjacket of Jewish ethnic identity and embrace people of every race. And because Luke chooses to tell us a story, we need to read his narrative incident by incident, asking ourselves: 'What does this tell us about God fulfilling his promise to Abraham?'

Acts begins with Luke reminding Theophilus that in his first volume he had told his patron what Jesus *began* to do and teach, the implication being that this second volume would be a continuation of what Jesus came to do. But now that Jesus was in heaven, he would be working through his disciples, the church. Just as Jesus had been empowered for his task by the Holy Spirit, so now was the church. The Spirit came so that the church could take the good news to all the earth (2:1–13).

The church preached as Jesus had done (e.g. 2:14–36; 3:12–26; 17:16–34). It also lived as he did, showing concern for the poor and marginalized, giving pride of place to praise and prayer, and being enabled by God to perform signs that demonstrated the truth of its message (2:42–47; 4:32–37). The church spread the message not just through what it said but also through what it did. The first public incident following the day of Pentecost involved Peter healing a lame man at the gate of the temple (Acts 3:1–26). Notice that Peter offered this man a chance to experience the new life the early Christians enjoyed before he taught him anything about Jesus: the good news was experienced before it was believed.

Having established that it is through the church that Jesus is continuing his work of bringing salvation to people through faith in him, Luke moves on to show how the church began to edge into the Gentile world. Luke stresses that on the day of Pentecost people from all over the world heard and received the message. But it's pretty clear that they were all practising Jews, whether born that way or having converted to Judaism from paganism (2:5–12).

The first move into the Gentile world came when God gave Peter a vision of animals that a good Jew wouldn't eat and invited him to dine (10:9–23). Peter saw the same vision three times, a conscious echo of his three-fold denial of Jesus. As soon as he had seen it, Gentiles called on Peter and he ate with them. The walls that divided Jew from Gentile were cracking. When God gave the Holy Spirit to Cornelius, the Gentile soldier, while Peter was explaining the message of Jesus, those walls came crashing to the ground, though it's clear from Galatians that Peter took a long time to come to terms with the shock of it (10:23–48; see Galatians 2:11–14).

The stoning of Stephen in Jerusalem had been followed by a great persecution against the church there (7:54 – 8:3), and believers fleeing from it had preached, gossipped and shared the gospel all the way up the coast to Antioch, where Gentiles came to faith in Jesus and believers were called Christians for the first time (11:19–31). No longer was the church just a sect within Judaism: it was breaking out and taking on a separate identity of its own. It is possible from the way Luke has structured his story that the church in Antioch was coming into being at the same time as Peter was having his life-changing encounter with Cornelius. The Holy Spirit was breaking out into the Gentile world on many fronts simultaneously.

That process was very painful. Luke records the debate that took place in Jerusalem between those who wanted to welcome the Gentiles with open arms and those who were insisting that the Gentiles become Jews before they became Christians. The so-called Jerusalem Council decreed that nothing should be put in the way of Gentiles' coming to faith in Christ. The fact was that God had shown that this was his will by giving the gift of the Holy Spirit to the Gentiles in almost the same way as he had given it to the original Jewish believers on the day of Pentecost (15:1–29).

Caterpillars become butterflies

It is hard to overstate the importance that Luke seems to attach to the church in Antioch. It is truly the church that broke the mould. Before chapter 11, where he tells us about the founding of the church, the thrust of his story had been on the progress of the gospel among the Jews. Afterwards, the focus shifts to the Gentile mission. Why? Because it appears that it was in Antioch that believers grasped the implications of the truth that people were saved only through Jesus and not by any religious or cultural observances such as circumcision, dietary laws and dress codes. It was in Antioch that the believers were first called 'Christians': here was a mixed group of Gentiles and Jews, identified not by an ethnic marker but solely in relation to their faith in Christ. And this was not something that these Christians took for granted. They recognized that it had to be fought for. And they were prepared to take on the might of the rather more conservative Jerusalem church to ensure that the vital truth that you don't have to be Jewish to be a Christian was established and accepted by all the churches (15:1–2).

The church at Antioch proved itself to be a mouldbreaker in another respect too, by the way. It was the first church to send missionaries (13:1–3). Up to this point, the church had grown somewhat haphazardly, helped mainly by the scattering of believers caused by persecution. The believers at Antioch realized that they were on to something so special – a message of new life and hope that united people across the deepest of ethnic hatreds – that the rest of the world just had to hear about it. So they sent Barnabas and Saul, two of their key leaders, to tell others in what is now Greece and Turkey about the wonderful news that had changed their lives.

After the Council, Luke's focus of attention shifts north from Antioch, the base for Paul's mission, to Turkey, Greece, Cyprus, Crete, Malta and Italy as the good news of Jesus was enthusiastically received by Gentiles all over the Empire. Indeed, while the Gentiles were flocking to hear and believe the gospel of a crucified Jewish healer and teacher, the Jews were getting decidedly frosty. Paul was hounded around the Near East by Jews seeking to have him silenced. And sadly, some Jewish Christians joined in (17:1–9).

But it seems the more he was opposed, the more Paul's mission saw success among the Gentiles, with churches being planted in many major cities between Antioch and Rome. Luke, it seems, is telling us in story form what Paul himself tells us in Romans 9 – 11: that God is using the mystery of Jewish unbelief to open his kingdom to the Gentiles and so to fulfil his promise to Abraham.

It wasn't that God had abandoned one lot of people, the Jews, and taken up with a new crowd, the Gentiles. That would hardly suggest that God is someone you can rely on. Rather, God was creating a new people out of his old people, much as a butterfly is created out of a caterpillar. His new people consisted of both Jews and Gentiles, united not by their ethnic origin, but by their faith in Christ and their sharing of the life of God through the Holy Spirit living within and among them.

Getting the point

'So you see, from Acts 2 it is clear that everyone must be baptized in the Spirit after they have been converted,' he said.

'Ah, but what about the conversion of Cornelius? He was baptized in the Holy Spirit before he repented or acknowledged Jesus as Lord,' she replied.

'Acts 6 clearly shows that churches should be run by deacons elected by the church members,' she asserted.

'Wait a minute,' he replied. 'Acts 14 and 19 clearly show that churches should be governed by elders appointed by apostles who are responsible for a number of churches.'

There's nothing quite like the Acts of the Apostles for causing disagreement among believers from different church traditions! The fact is that each of the statements above is based on an episode in Acts, but none of them is true. The problem is that these incidents are being taken out of the context of Luke's story and used for something that wasn't in his mind when he wrote them down.

Acts 2 is the story of a unique event: the first coming of the Holy Spirit on the church. It is not the pattern for conversion. Neither is the story of Cornelius, the first Gentile believer. Acts 6 has nothing at all to do with deacons in the modern Baptist or Free Church sense of that title, and Acts 14 and 19 aren't much of a guide for contemporary house churches.

The point is that Luke didn't write Acts to tell us how the church was organized. He isn't very interested in the nitty-gritty, day-to-day running of the church. He certainly isn't laying down a pattern that must be followed by Christians in every age.

The Seven appointed in Acts 6, for instance, are never called deacons, and exercise most of their ministry away from the Jerusalem church that appointed them. Luke never tells us how or why James, Jesus' brother (who hadn't believed in Jesus prior to the crucifixion), came to be the leader of the church in Jerusalem. He doesn't tell us that every church established by Paul was run the same way.

People who come to Acts because they want to find out how to get back to the New Testament church are in for a big disappointment. There just isn't enough information. Luke's intention is for us to see what happened and who was behind it. God was gathering his people, in accordance with his promise to Abraham, from the Jewish world and the Gentile world. The agent he was using was the church, and the means was the preaching of the good news of Jesus, inspired by the Holy Spirit, who also demonstrated the truth of the message in people's lives.

If Acts contains a model or pattern for us to follow it is this: the church in every generation exists to proclaim the gospel of Jesus Christ to people of all nations. If it does that, it will be inspired and led by the Spirit of Jesus, who operates through the lives of believers, bringing unbelievers to an awareness of the truth of the gospel. The goal of this should be to create communities drawn from every nation and united by a common faith in Jesus. As to organization and methods, Luke's message is this: whatever works to achieve this goal and is in line with the message and the Spirit of Jesus is OK.

Questions

1. Acts is a record of how the church spread around the ancient world. Then, as now, the church ran into problems. Read 6:1–7; 11:1–18; 15:1–35. What do we learn about:
   (a) how to resolve conflicts between believers?
   (b) how the church can deal with racism in its own structures and thus be a beacon to the world on this sensitive, vital issue?
2. How can we build inclusive communities that attract people by the quality of our relationships as the early Christian communities did (see 2:42–47; 4:32–37; 11:19–30)?
3. How was Antioch a mould-breaking church? What lessons can we learn from it for our own churches (11:19–30; 13:1–3; 14:24 – 15:2, 30–35)?

4

Just what is it God has done?

Romans, Galatians, Colossians

How much TV will you watch this week? Why not reduce it by half an hour a night? If you drop a soap opera, a makeover show and one quiz, you'll have plenty of time to read this chapter and Galatians, Romans and Colossians. To get caught up in the drama of Paul's good news, why not read each of the letters through once on days 2–5? Alternatively, follow the plan below.

Day 1 Read this chapter.
Day 2 Read Galatians 1 – 6.
Day 3 Read Romans 1 – 11.
Day 4 Read Romans 12 – 16.
Day 5 Read Colossians 1 – 4.
Day 6 Re-read this chapter and look at the discussion questions.
Day 7 Meet with the friends you are reading this book with, have a meal or a drink, and talk through the discussion questions and anything else that struck you through your reading.

Although Luke wrote more words, the theological heart of the our New Testament comes from the pen of Paul of Tarsus, the Pharisee turned church-planter who spearheaded the Christian faith's thrust into the Gentile world and became its first significant theologian (see chapter 21).

Our next four chapters look at Paul's thirteen letters.

It is impossible in so short a space to do justice to all that is contained in each of these startling pieces of writing. So our aim is to focus on the dominant theme in each letter. We'll start by looking at the gospel Paul preached. This is *the* major topic of all his writing, so we'll start by concentrating on what Romans, Galatians and Colossians tell us about the basic framework of his teaching. Then in subsequent chapters we can flesh out that picture in relation to other key Christian themes. We'll look at what Paul says about the church (chapter 5), spirituality and hope (chapter 6) and Christian relationships (chapter 7).

The heart of the matter

Galatians is probably Paul's earliest letter (1 Thessalonians is the other contender) and Romans one of his later ones. But both argue the same basic point, though in a somewhat different tone of voice. These are the letters that give us the clearest exposition of Paul's key theological ideas. What is the good news he proclaimed around the Gentile world? In Romans he declared that this gospel demands the obedience of everyone everywhere (1:5); in Galatians he was amazed that his first readers were abandoning it (1:6–7). Just what was the big deal?

Most people, if they have a view on Romans at all, reckon it's about 'justification by faith', how God puts us right with himself through Jesus. Such a view couldn't be more wrong. The problem with it is that it reduces Paul's greatest letter, undoubtedly the most remarkable piece of Christian theology ever penned, to a tract about how I get to heaven when I die. And important though that topic is to each of us, God's plans and Paul's gospel are about much more.

Romans addresses the crucial issue that confronted the first Christians: do you have to be a Jew to be part of the people of God? Paul's answer was an emphatic 'no'. And the theology behind that answer, laid out in both Galatians and Romans, demonstrates that the gospel is about how God is redeeming the whole world, putting right what people have wrecked through their sin and rebellion against their creator and calling all people, whether Jew or Gentile, to worship the one true God and join him in his mission to save the planet. It is a truly global message.

Famous first drafts ...

Galatians, one of the angriest letters in the New Testament, was written in the heat of the moment, probably in the months leading up to the Jerusalem Council that would debate the inclusion of Gentiles in the church (Acts 15). It speaks about how the gospel sets us free from patterns of religion tied to ethnic identity and creates a community of equals drawn from every nation and social grouping. Its message is as revolutionary today as when it left Paul's pen.

The Galatian churches were overwhelmingly Gentile, planted as a result of Paul's first missionary journey with Barnabas (Acts 13 – 14). Luke tells us that on the return leg of that journey, Paul encouraged his new converts to remain true to the faith and warned them of hardships that would surely come their way (Acts 14:22–23). They weren't long in coming. Acts 15:1 tells us that people came to Antioch insisting that Gentile converts had to keep the law of Moses – that is, get circumcised (if they were blokes), give up pork and observe the Sabbath. These messengers (*Judaizers*, so called because they were insisting that Gentile believers should become Jews) were peddling their wares everywhere Paul and Barnabas had been, and having rather more success in Galatia than in Antioch (Acts 15:2; Galatians 1:6).

In haste, Paul dashed off Galatians, a letter that lacks the customary niceties of extended greetings and a report of how Paul was praying for his readers. Instead he launches straight in, laying out his credentials and authority as a messenger of Jesus Christ, reiterating the core of the good news he preached to them and blasting his opponents out of the water.

Galatians is a charter of freedom. Paul asserts that the good news sets everyone free from the spiritual forces that seek to control and manipulate our lives, including sin and religion. It all started with Abraham, he says, whom God called to be the founder of a family that related to him through faith and faith alone (Genesis 12; Galatians 3:1–29). Through this family, God pledged that he would reclaim the world and rescue it from all the effects and penalties of sin. This promise was fulfilled in Jesus on the cross, where he trounced the forces that held the world in thrall to sin and slavery. So to get on board with what God was doing in the world, you needed to have faith in Jesus (2:15–16). That was the gospel – good news to both Jew and Gentile.

The complicating factor in the first century was the existence of the nation of Israel, Abraham's legitimate ethnic family. For over a thousand years, it had been the carrier of the promise to Abraham. It had been given the law, a guide to behaviour for the people of God. It had been given a covenant by which God had made forgiveness of sins possible through the sacrifice of substitute animals, especially those offered annually on the Day of Atonement. Israel was not accepted by God because it kept the law. Israel kept and valued the law because it was accepted by God, who had chosen them, rescued them from slavery in Egypt and made his covenant with them at Sinai (*en route* to freedom in the promised land), all because of his promise to Abraham. The problem was that Israel had forgotten its calling to be a light to the rest of the world; it assumed that God was interested in them alone and not in being God to all the other nations.

Paul's argument in Galatians is that the covenant with Abraham came first and sets the agenda for what God wants to do with the world. It came before circumcision and before the law of Moses and before the establishment of Israel. It is the primary covenant, the one based on promise and grace and entered by faith – Abraham's faith in the first instance (Genesis 15:6; Galatians 3:6–9). The law of Moses, according to Galatians, functioned like a schoolteacher, keeping the people on the straight and narrow and instructing them in the things of God, before God fulfilled his promise to Abraham and sent a Saviour who would deal once and for all with the problem of sin and create a people drawn from every nation of the world, who related to God solely on the basis of faith.

This is what Paul had taught the Gentiles of Galatia. This was the message that persuaded them to turn from pagan idolatry to serve the one true God who had sent his Son Jesus to die for them and through whom they had received the gift of the Holy Spirit (3:1–5). But once Paul had left, the Judaizers came, preaching a gospel that said: 'If you want to be a Christian, you've got to become a Jew first.'

They did this for two reasons. One was a misunderstanding of God's covenant with Israel: they assumed the priority of Sinai over Abraham, which Paul shows is wrong. The second was their quite understandable fear that if the law were ditched as a guiding principle for God's people, morality and godly behaviour would go out of the window. But Paul said that the Spirit would guard against that.

Approaching Galatians

With this overview in mind, how should we approach our reading of Galatians? The letter falls fairly tidily into three equal sections, the middle one being by far the most complex.

Chapters 1 and 2 lay out Paul's credentials as a messenger of the true gospel of freedom in opposition to those who would bind the Galatians to a mountain of religious rules and regulations. He introduces the key theme: God has dealt with sin through Jesus on the cross and we relate to God by faith plus nothing else (1:1, 4; 2:20–21; see also 3:1, 13; 4:4–5; 5:1, 11, 24; 6:12, 14). This is vital, because Paul believed that the Judaizers robbed the cross of its significance by insisting that people should follow the law of Moses as well as the crucified Messiah.

Through the cross, says Paul, we have moved from the present evil age, controlled by malign forces, to the new age of the Messiah and his kingdom that would one day fill the whole world (1:3, 4:3, 8–9; 6:15; see Colossians 2:8; Ephesians 2:1-2; see also 'King of the hill' on pages 56–57). Through the cross, he says, we have also been set free from sin and religious striving. For these Galatian Gentiles to submit to the law of Moses was to take on a yoke of slavery identical to the pagan one they'd left when they first came to faith.

Paul demonstrates the truth of this by telling his own story and by asserting that his message is the same as that believed and preached by the other leading apostles (1:11–2:21). It is entirely possible that the Judaizers had persuaded the Galatians that they represented the 'true' faith of the mother church in Jerusalem.

But it wasn't enough for Paul to assert, however loudly, that he was right and his opponents were wrong. He also had to demonstrate their error by arguing from the Old Testament, because they had come claiming that the Bible was on their side, not on Paul's. In chapters 3 and 4, Paul shows how wrong they are.

In chapter 3 he leads us through a complex, tightly argued and truly wonderful Bible study based on Genesis 15 and Deuteronomy 27 – 30. It focuses on four words: *Christ*, *covenant*, *curse* and *community*. Paul demonstrates two things. First, God's intention had always been to create one family (community) out of all the nations of the earth, of which Abraham was the father and model (3:6–9, 14, 16–17, 26, 29). Entry into that family was by faith (3:6–9, 11, quoting Habbakuk 2:4). Secondly, Israel was intended to be a stepping-stone to this goal, but had become a stumbling-block because of its sin and insularity.

At the heart of this Bible study (3:10–13) Paul asserts that Israel is under a curse because of its unfaithfulness to God. Deuteronomy 27 – 30 had warned Israel that its sin would lead to exile. And though Israel had physically returned to the land, spiritually the exile had never really ended; the great prophecies of life after the exile in Deuteronomy 30, Isaiah 65 and Jeremiah 31 had not yet been fulfilled.

But, says Paul, on the cross, Jesus, as Israel's true king and representative, bore the punishment for Israel's sin (and the sin of the whole world), so that the curse could be lifted and a new community of people relating to God through faith in Jesus could come into being; a single community drawn from every nation worshipping the one true God. And the life of the new age, spelled out in those great Old Testament prophecies, could begin (1:4).

In chapter 4, he contrasts the line of descent from Abraham through Isaac and Ishmael, suggesting that Christians are heirs of the freeborn son, Isaac, while the Judaizers are heirs of the slave, Ishmael (4:21–31; see 3:26–29). In this he reinforces his contention that freedom comes not from religious observance but through faith in Jesus. To follow the Judaizers, he says in no uncertain terms, leads directly to slavery, misery and oppression (4:8–20).

Then in chapters 5 and 6 he spells out how this freedom is lived out in the world in the power of the Spirit. In a breath-taking description of the Christian life, he describes how the Spirit grows in the believer the qualities needed to live together in the new family God is creating through Jesus (5:16–26; on this see chapter 5), and then suggests some ways in which those qualities will ensure that we live together in peace, watching over one another in love (6:1–10).

As well as anger, there is deep and passionate concern for the believers of Galatia in this letter. Paul likens himself to their mother, distraught at their waywardness, longing for them to know the freedom and wholeness that come from the true gospel (3:19–20).

Famous last words

The controversy addressed by Galatians rumbled on for most of Paul's life. Having mentioned it in nearly all his letters, he addressed it in depth in his letter to the church at Rome. One scholar has described Romans as Paul's last will and testament. This is a bit of an exaggeration, but it does capture something of the tone of the letter.

It was written in the spring of AD 57. Paul is in Corinth waiting to take the gift he has collected among his Gentile congregations to Jerusalem to give it to James and the Jewish believers (15:25–29). He knows that the journey he is about to undertake is full of risk (see Acts 21:1–15), but he is determined to take it and is already planning what he might do when this phase of his ministry is complete. His thoughts turn west to Rome and beyond, and so, with half an eye on the past but one and a half on the future, he writes to the Christians at Rome.

There are probably three major reasons why Paul wrote. First, he was planning a mission to Spain, and Rome would have been a good launchpad for such a venture. Further west than Corinth, his current centre of operations, it had an established Christian church from which he could draw support (15:18–24). It is worth noting, however, that Paul was almost certainly not asking the Romans for money to fund his mission. The costs of that were being picked up by Phoebe, among others.

Secondly, Paul wanted to write a defence of his ministry, a statement for posterity, if you like. After all, why should the Roman churches have anything to do with this man from the east of the Empire with a mixed and controversial reputation? Paul is writing not an abstract thesis about the gospel in general but a statement about his ministry – a Jewish Pharisee's gospel for Gentiles. He wants to outline his understanding of what God is up to in the world (1:16; 3:8; 9:1–2). And the style of his writing, especially his habit of asking rhetorical questions to further his argument (e.g. 6:1, 15; 7:7; etc.), shows that he is only too well aware that his message will be contentious in a church comprising both Jews and Gentiles.

So he writes to spell out and defend his take on the good news of how, through Jesus, Jews and Gentiles are coming together to form a new people of God, based not on ethnic origin, or on performing certain religious acts that mark them off from other people, but on faith in Jesus. And he doesn't just write an intellectual defence. He makes it clear all through his letter that it is only this gospel that unleashes the power of God to change both people and the world they live in (1:16–17; 15:17–21).

Thirdly, Paul wrote to address the pastoral needs of a mixed Christian community. The church in Rome was made up of a number of congregations from different ethnic, social and religious backgrounds. The greetings in chapter 16 show that there were slaves as well as members of the imperial household; there were merchants and traders, rich and poor, Jews and Gentiles, women and men, black and white. (See *Discovering Romans*, page 224.)

Paul's message addressed the very real problem of unity between all these disparate groups. For him the only source of that unity could be the message of Jesus, the gospel of the cross and the resurrection, the good news that God was calling one people out of all the nations of the world. This is the theme of Romans 1 – 11. In chapters 12 – 15, he spells out how we live together in unity despite our diverse backgrounds.

Reading through Romans

Bearing in mind why Romans was written, we'll take a whistle-stop tour through the letter before coming back to show how its greeting and benediction encapsulate the major theme of Paul's gospel.

Having introduced himself and his theme (1:1-17), Paul launches into an analysis of the human condition. Everyone has sinned, he says, whether Gentile (1:18–32) or Jew (2:1–29). We have all rebelled against our creator, and thus are all under the curse that comes as a punishment for sin (3:1–20). In Galatians Paul had talked about the curse in terms of exile. In Romans, too, this is the effect that sin has: people are alienated; they have nowhere to call home.

The good news is that sin has met its match in Jesus Christ, God's Son, Israel's king who now rules on high (3:21 – 4:25; cf. 1:2–6). Paul describes the cross as a cosmic Day of Atonement which, once and for all time, dealt with the consequences of the human race's rebellion against its creator (3:21–26). Through the cross, both Jew and Gentile find a place in God's new people (3:27–31). Through the cross God fulfils his promise to Abraham (4:1–25). The good news marks a new beginning for individuals (5:1–11) and for the human race (5:12–21). The key point is that Christ's death marks a new start for the whole world. The tragedy of

Adam, which affects all of humanity, has been met by the triumph of Jesus, which likewise affects the whole human race.

Romans 1:18 – 5:21 compares and contrasts two humanities – one 'in Adam' and the other 'in Christ' – showing how God has dealt with the problem of sin that affects all humanity and how the salvation that has been made possible through the cross of Christ is available to all who are in Adam: that is to say, the whole human race. Membership of the people of God, which hitherto had been restricted to those ethnically related to Abraham (the Jews), is now open to all who have faith in Jesus, regardless of ethnicity.

Something decisive and life-changing has happened, but that 'something' has yet to be completed. Paul now turns to deal with the issues that we all face in the life of faith: the problem of sin (6:1–23); the problem of the law, which those who promote its continuing relevance for the Christian believer say is a bulwark against sin (7:1–25); the problem of our old nature and impending death; and the relationship of our salvation to the redemption of the whole created order (8:1–39).

This discussion raises an equally acute problem: what about ethnic Israel? If both Jew and Gentile are saved through faith in Christ, where does this leave the Old Testament people of God? Paul deals with this vexed and, for him, heart-breaking problem in chapters 9 – 11. Here he argues that in the gospel God demonstrates his faithfulness to his promises, especially his promise to Abraham that he will save for himself a people out of every nation of the world. 'All Israel' (11:26), therefore, is the totality of God's people, Jew and Gentile, saved through the cross of Christ. Paul's argument in these chapters is difficult, but seems to hinge on the fact that Jewish unbelief and rejection of Jesus have opened the door to the Gentiles and mysteriousiy furthered God's plans.

It's all very well to gather people of all types into one family, but this can and does lead to tensions and disputes. Paul is always keen to stress that what Christians believe ought to be seen in the way they live. This theme is doubly important in this letter: having redefined Israel and asserted that Christ is the end (that is, fulfilment) of the law (10:4), he has to show how godly living is possible apart from the law (much as he did in Galatians). So he speaks of offering ourselves to God (12:1–2) and then about living together in the community of faith (12:3–8), including how the Spirit empowers us for such a life, before going on to stress that love is the norm for all our relationships (12:9–21), even in public and social life (13:1–10) – seen, for instance, in paying our taxes (13:6–7)!

Then he turns his attention to specific issues that would have tested the love of this mixed group of believers. What about those who observe special diets and holy days (14:1 – 15:6)? We should not be divided over matters of preference, he says; meat-eaters versus vegetarians, teetotallers versus drinkers, swingers from chandeliers versus adherents of the 1662 Prayer Book. These are things we like doing, and might even find helpful to our faith, but which are not part of the gospel message.

Then 15:7–13 sums up all the theology and ethics of the letter. Christ the Jew is the Gentiles' Saviour. God's faithfulness to the Jews has opened the door of salvation to Gentiles, so Israel now consists of any and all who have faith in Jesus. Some have even suggested, with a degree of plausibility, that 15:7 is the key text in Romans and the point of the whole letter.

Paul's story and God's story

The other contender for key text is 1:16. But in fact 1:1–6 is even more crucial, because it roots Paul's message in the unfolding story of God's love affair with the world. Here Paul tells us that what follows in this letter is the story of a man (verse 3) who was God (verse 4); a Jew who is now Lord of Gentiles as well as Jews – greater and more powerful than Caesar who claimed that title (verse 4c); the one through whom the creator of the world comes to claim the allegiance of all the peoples of the world, as prophesied by the Old Testament (especially Isaiah 40 – 66; verse 2).

More than that: this story is now Paul's story. He has been caught up in the adventure of the gospel. He is God's herald, proclaiming the reign of the Messiah, Jesus, and commanding the world to bow the knee to its true king (verses 1, 5). And even more than this: it is our story. Through faith we have become a part of God's plan to redeem the world and reclaim what was snatched away from him by humanity's rebellion.

In these opening verses Paul asserts that what follows is not merely about our personal salvation; it is about global redemption and God taking his rightful place as king of all that he has made.

And just in case we've missed this focus on our way through this long and at times difficult text, Paul reminds us of this story at the end of his letter; and he does so in the only proper context: worship (16:25–27).

God's plans for the world, so long shrouded in mystery, have now been revealed in a new work of prophecy (verses 25b–26a). Paul is claiming that this letter is a prophetic writing in the sense that it spells out God's grand design for the world he made (see also on Ephesians in chapter 5). That design focuses on Jesus (verse 25b) and God's call that all people from all nations serve him (verse 26b). More than that, the plan is unfolding now through the gospel Paul preaches (verse 25a). You can almost hear the great apostle echoing the words of Hannibal Smith of the *A Team*: 'I just love it when a plan comes together.' No wonder Paul explodes in praise (verses 25a, 27).

King of the hill

But the good news about Jesus didn't just have global consequences. It was even bigger than that. As Paul showed the Colossian Christians, this message affected life in the spiritual as well as the material realm: allegiance to Jesus meant renouncing the claims that other gods made over you. This was and still is a major step for anyone to take.

Paul's world was a place where people were acutely

aware not just of the material world but also of the spiritual realm that exercised a very real influence over daily life. There were gods and goddesses that controlled everything from trade to travel, sex to salvation, wine to wisdom. To live well, you needed to ensure that these powers were on your side and that you did nothing to upset them.

When Paul wrote to the Colossian Christians from his Roman jail in the early 60s, he wrote to a group of people who were beginning to come under the sway of teachers who suggested that as well as putting our trust in Jesus, maybe we needed the help of some of these other spiritual powers. After all, they might be able to supply wisdom and power for living that Jesus couldn't.

Colossians is a stinging rebuke to such teachers. At its heart is a portrait of Jesus as king of the hill. He is Lord of the spiritual realms as well as of the material world; he is the suffering Messiah who, on the cross, triumphed over the forces that keep the world in fearful thrall.

The centrepiece of Colossians is a magnificent poem in which Paul paints a breathtaking picture of the ruler of the universe (1:15–20). Here Paul asserts that Jesus is Lord of the powers (as he is of all things) because he made them. These forces have nothing to teach those who are redeemed by Christ and filled with his Spirit (1:21–23), for it is Jesus who has all wisdom and knowledge (2:2–4), not the powers.

Indeed, Jesus has disarmed the powers, stripped them of any claim they might have to our allegiance and held them up to public ridicule (2:15). He did this so that they could no longer hold people in bondage to their petty rules and regulations, and so that they could no longer rob people of the chance to experience life in all its fullness. The false teachers, says Paul, are selling slavery; Christ is offering freedom.

Therefore, he says, we should stay rooted in Christ (2:6) and resist hollow and deceptive philosophy. There's nothing to be gained from being a slave to such stuff, says Paul, and much to be lost. Then Paul goes on to show how Christians should live in the world in the light of Christ's cosmic victory over the powers (3:1 – 4:6). Jesus sets the agenda for Christian living (3:1–5). In our behaviour we bow the knee to him alone, not to the prevailing public mood, the ruling political powers or the fads and fashions of the day. If we do this we shall be free and able to live with one another, and hence testify to the reality of Christ's victory to the world. (See on Ephesians, pages 62–64, for a fuller exposition of this.)

Questions

1. What has God achieved in Christ? How would you describe it to someone who has never heard of Jesus?
2. What works of the law do modern Christians impose on each other? How does Galatians help us to resist?
3. 'Romans is about justification by faith.' Do you agree, or not? (Answer with reference to the whole text of Romans, not just chapter 3.)
4. How does the teaching of Romans and Galatians help us to forge multiracial, multicultural church communities in the twenty-first century?
5. Read Colossians 1:15–20. What does this poem tell us about God and about Jesus? (It might help you to read the poem forwards, from verse 15 to verse 20, and then backwards, from verse 20 to verse 15. Doing this will open up a fresh understanding of the relationship between God and Jesus.)

Why is it so hard to live together?

Ephesians, 1 and 2 Corinthians

The drama hots up this week. What happens when people get caught up in Paul's good news? What does a community of Christians look like? Why does it fail so often and so painfully? Now we're hooked, our aim is to read this chapter and Ephesians and 1 and 2 Corinthians. You can either follow the plan below or read all the texts being studied right through each day on days 2–5.

Day 1 Read this chapter.
Day 2 Read Ephesians 1 – 6.
Day 3 Read 1 Corinthians 1 – 10.
Day 4 Read 1 Corinthians 11 – 16; 2 Corinthians 1 – 5.
Day 5 Read 2 Corinthians 6 – 13.
Day 6 Re-read this chapter and look at the discussion questions.
Day 7 Meet with the friends you are reading this book with, have a meal or a drink, and talk through the discussion questions and anything else that struck you through your reading.

People often say, 'If only we could get back to the New Testament church, all our problems would be solved.' Such people are not reading the same New Testament as I am. For the church we encounter in Paul's letters is frequently riven with in-fighting and division, troubled by dodgy teaching and run by overbearing leaders. It's also a place where sinners are finding new life and where communities are being transformed by God's Holy Spirit. In fact, it's just like every church I've ever had dealings with.

Paul has a lot to say about the church because most of his letters were written to specific Christian communities to deal with the particular problems they were facing in living together as God's new people in Christ. The church at Corinth, with whom he had a roller-coaster relationship for over a decade, and to whom he wrote a number of letters, provides the clearest example of how the apostle dealt with the nitty-gritty of church life in the raw. By contrast, his letter to the Ephesians gives us his clearest theology of what the church should be and how it fits into God's plans for his world. And that's where we'll begin.

God's grand design

Ephesians was almost certainly written at the same time as Colossians, and shares that letter's eagle's-eye view of God's strategy in human history and where the church fits into it. But unlike Colossians, with which it shares many features, Ephesians does not seem to have been addressing pressing problems in a specific church. Maybe because it was written from prison (probably Rome in the early 60s), Paul had more time to reflect on the big picture and how the kind of teaching he was tailoring to meet the needs of the Colossian Christians could be generalized to help all Christians to grasp God's grand design and live more effectively and harmoniously together. So, although addressed to the Ephesians, it's likely that the letter was intended for all the churches in the Lycus valley that Tychicus passed by *en route* from Ephesus, where he landed, to Colosse, to which he was travelling with Onesimus to deliver Colossians and Philemon (Colossians 4:7–9; Ephesians 6:21–22).

Ephesians has a truly cosmic scope. It deals with the 'heavenly places' (1:3, 10, 20; 2:6; 3:10; 6:12) and with 'things on earth' (1:10; 3:15; 4:9; 6:3). And it shows how Jesus is the focus of God's dealings with both these spheres, which represent the whole of the created order. It is through Jesus that harmony, wrecked by both heavenly and human rebellion, is restored. Indeed, the main theme of Ephesians, spelled out in 1:9–10, is how, through Jesus, God is bringing everything back to unity and to the wholeness God had always intended it to have. Having spelled this out in cosmic terms in chapter 1, Paul goes on to show how the church is the visible example that this reunification of all things has begun.

From before he could remember, Paul had recited the *Shema* (Deuteronomy 6:4) every day. (*Shema* is Hebrew for 'Hear!') This basic tenet of Jewish faith reminded Paul that God was one and that he had no peer or rival. Further, he had created the world in harmony and balance (Genesis 1 – 2), but, through a series of rebellions, that harmony had been ruptured (Genesis 3 – 11). In hope, Paul had recited the *Shema* knowing that one day the unity destroyed by the fall would be restored, that God would indeed once again become king of all things and that the creation would once again be restored to peace and wholeness under his sovereign rule (Zechariah 14:9, a theme taken up in many of the apocalyptic writings Paul would have studied; see chapters 16 and 20).

Now, as he begins this letter, he praises God that what he had longed for was starting to happen. In Christ the harmony of creation was being restored. It was seen as individuals came into a relationship with their creator through Jesus; God was truly becoming king over people from all nations, not just Israel. Supremely it was seen in the church (1:22–23; 2:11–22).

In Paul's understanding, God's plan to unite all things in Christ would happen 'in the fullness of time' (1:10). This idea, drawn from the apocalyptic writings, looked forward to a time when God would decisively step in and sort things out; when the present evil age would be ended, and the age to come, the age of justice and joy, would be ushered in. Now, in Christ, says Paul, that time has come. But instead of one age ending and a new one beginning, the new age – the age of the kingdom of God – has begun before the old one has ended. We live in the overlap between these two ages.

Paul asserts, then, that God's plan to unite all things in Christ has been revealed but not yet completed. How do we know this isn't just wishful thinking? Two reasons, says Paul. The first is that we've experienced the Holy Spirit who has come into our lives and is changing us as a result of our faith in Jesus (1:11–14). The second, which proves that what is happening is more than just a personal experience of something divine, is the church. The church, in which men and women of all backgrounds and races find a place, is proof that God's plan to unite all things in Christ has begun. And the key evidence Paul produces to demonstrate this is that in the church Jew and Gentile are being united (2:11–22).

Indeed, in Ephesians 2 Paul asserts that the one God (Deuteronomy 6:4) is creating one new person (2:14–15 – the Greek word rendered 'humanity' is *anthrōpos*, 'human being') as proof that his plan to unite all things is under way. To begin with, he talks about our individual lives before and after coming to faith in Jesus, culminating in the fact that this has happened so that we may do the good works God has prepared for us (2:1–10). Then he spells out the context within which we experience this new life and do our good works: namely, the church. The new person spoken of in 2:14–15 is the product of God's reconciling work through Christ (2:12–14). God is creating a single humanity out of all the nations of the earth. Whereas the old humanity was divided by culture and race, and especially, for Paul, by the works of the law that marked Jew off from Gentile (2:11), the new humanity is united in Christ. In the church, says Paul, God is creating a third race – not Jew, not Gentile, but Christian (cf. Acts 11:26c).

The best-kept secret

This is 'the mystery' that Paul speaks of (3:2–6), the message he preached (3:7–9) and the message the church preaches through its existence as well as through its works and words (3:10–13). Where's the evidence of God's grand design? In the church. This is evidence for both the heavenly and earthly realms, because the church is the basis of the new community that will characterize life in the new heaven and new earth once God's plan has been fulfilled.

It is important at this point to recognize that the heavenly places Paul speaks of are not a realm separate from life on earth. The phrase refers to the unseen world of spiritual reality. That is to say, it is the whole of the here and now, not just the bits we can see. The heavenly places are where Christ reigns supreme (1:20–21), where the principalities and powers operate (3:10; 6:12), and where God provides all we need now to live as he wants us to (1:3–4; see *Discovering Ephesians*, pp. 99–100).

This is so mind-blowing that Paul prays that his readers will be able to grasp it (3:14–21). Notice that Paul picks up the theme of unity by referring to God as the Father of the whole family in both heaven and earth (verses 14–15). Paul prays that we'll be able to fathom out what God is up to. In verse 18 the focus is not on 'love' (the word doesn't appear in that verse) but on the grand design. It is so big that we really can't get our heads round it. But it is written in love (verse 19) so that we may experience it even if we can't comprehend it. And we certainly won't grasp it on our own. We need all the saints to help us; we need each other's insights and wisdom (3:18).

The rest of the letter is devoted to how we should live in the church to ensure that God's grand design is made a visible reality in our communities. Paul starts by stressing our unity and our responsibility to maintain it (4:1–6) and then outlining how Christ has given us the resources we need to do that (4:7–16). Notice, in passing, how Paul sets the gifts in the context of Christ's cosmic victory over the powers (a theme that dominates Colossians; see pages 56–58) which reinforces the point that the church demonstrates God's wisdom to the powers (3:10) and refutes the notion prevalent in the Lycus valley that the powers can help the church to do its work.

Paul then spells out in practical terms how these gifts and

our life in the church help us to live as witnesses to God's grand design both at home and at work (4:17 – 6:9). Finally, he warns us that God's plan will be opposed (6:10–19). If the church is visible proof of God's plan to unite all things in Christ, then God's enemies, both human and spiritual, will attack it. So we need to arm ourselves against the onslaught of rebellious heavenly forces that use things on earth (such as persecution, political pressure, imprisonment and divisions between Christians) to destroy the church's witness to God's plan. Like Paul, we live to make the mystery known through our life together and our work and witness in the world (6:10–20).

Back to reality

'It's all very well for Paul to wax lyrical about God's grand design and how the church is evidence of all things coming together in Christ. He hasn't suffered a Sunday in my church; he doesn't have to put up with the backbiting and pettiness, the squabbling leadership and selfish "What's-in-it-for-me?" membership that I do!'

Wrong. Paul was involved in possibly the most dysfunctional church in history, a church so messed up you'd have thought the only thing to do with it was to tear it down and start again.

Paul had founded the church in Corinth in around AD 50 (Acts 18:1–17). During the course of an extended stay (Acts 18:11), he helped to create a vibrant, lively, multiracial fellowship in the city. When he left, the church was still a bit of an unruly teenager, but he had no way of knowing just how delinquent the church would turn out to be.

He wrote at least four times to this increasingly troublesome congregation. The first letter, offering general encouragement and advice on specific issues, is referred to in 1 Corinthians 5:9. Clearly, it was misunderstood because by the time Paul met some people from one of the Corinthian house churches, things were not good. The church was divided, its worship was chaotic, it was turning a blind eye to immorality and, because some of its teachers appeared to be from another planet, it had got the wrong end of the stick on some key Christian doctrines – notably the resurrection. (For more on this, read the introduction in *Discovering 2 Corinthians.*)

In a quest for guidance, some people from the church wrote to Paul. So he wrote again, from Ephesus in around AD 54 – the letter we have as 1 Corinthians. He intended to follow this letter up with a lengthy visit (1 Corinthians 16:5–12). But outsiders – possibly the same kind of Judaizers who had dogged Paul's tracks before – arrived in Corinth, challenging Paul's credentials. Timothy, whom Paul had sent ahead of his own visit, couldn't cope and left Corinth to join Paul in Ephesus. Paul sent off a stinging rocket of a letter that aimed to re-establish his authority (referred to in 2 Corinthians 2:4 and 7:8, and known as the 'severe' or 'painful' letter).

It seems that he almost immediately regretted it. He felt that he had been hasty, too harsh; that he had destroyed whatever relationship with Corinth he had left. But he got news from Titus (2 Corinthians 2:12–14) which sounded promising. So he wrote again. This fourth letter, which we know as 2 Corinthians, is an intensely personal defence of his ministry, an outpouring of joy at his restored relationship with the Corinthians and a vicious attack on his opponents all wrapped up in a theology of reconciliation through suffering. It is indeed a heady brew.

Finally, Paul arrived in Corinth (Acts 20:2), and it appears that harmony had broken out. Indeed, the church became his base for a while. He wrote Romans there while waiting to set sail for Jerusalem with the gift from the Gentile churches of Asia and Europe.

There are two things to note as we come to this lively correspondence. The first is that both letters were written out of the intense and difficult relationship Paul had with this church. There's very little abstract theology or general teaching in these letters. Paul did not sit down and think, 'Oh, I know, I'll tell them about spiritual gifts and the resurrection; I'll make a few comments about women and marriage and remind them to take up a collection.' All the teaching is born out of a twin desire to correct dangerous misunderstandings of the Christian life prevalent in the church and to re-establish his authority as a teacher in the church, which had been attacked from within and without.

Secondly, Paul wrote to the whole church, not just to the leaders – and certainly not to his opponents. The problems tearing the Corinthian church apart had to be faced and solved by the whole church coming together to listen to, weigh up and act on the apostle's words to them. It would be no good Paul urging the leaders who'd remained loyal to him to get tough with those who resisted Paul's version of the gospel. Rather, the whole church had to decide who was right. After all, it was when the church was gathered together that it could know the mind of Christ and hence chart a way forward out of the crisis engulfing it (1 Corinthians 2:6–16).

All human life is here

By the time Paul wrote 1 Corinthians, the church was in a mess. But this isn't really surprising. After all, this motley bunch of mainly Gentile converts came from a background of pagan excess and were living in a city whose name was a byword for sexual immorality of all kinds. This fledgling church was surrounded by powerful pagan cults in a society where religious and civic life was so closely intertwined it was hard to know when a religious act ended and a political, social or economic one began. This culture spilled over into the church as the new believers struggled with immorality, a litigious disposition and confusion about marriage, gender and whether to buy meat that had been offered to idols.

But the church had deeper problems. It was split over what the Christian faith was really all about. Some contended that the resurrection had already happened, so they could do what they liked. Others linked spirituality to an extreme asceticism that forbade sex even within marriage. At root, they struggled with the tension of the 'now' and 'not yet' of the Christian life (see chapter 16).

Scholars speak of the church succumbing to an 'over-realized eschatology' – which is as painful as it sounds. It means that their troubles stemmed from their belief that the kingdom had already arrived in all its fullness. This led many of the Corinthians to believe that they could do anything, that they were already kings (4:8), and that they had 'knowledge' that allowed them to judge for themselves what was right and wrong (see 6:12–19; 8:1–3; 10:23–24).

Somehow, Paul had to capture everyone's attention and turn their eyes back to the basics of the gospel, so that the church could rid itself of error and learn to live with diversity and difference within the unity that comes from faith in Christ.

He therefore reminds them that the good news is about Christ crucified (1:18 – 2:5). In the midst of a call to unity, addressed to a church tearing itself apart over which of its many patrons – Paul, Peter, Apollos – was the most gifted, dynamic, charismatic and eloquent leader (chapters 1 – 4), Paul turns their eyes back to the crucified Jesus. This hanged man is the measure of God's wisdom, the standard against which all leadership – indeed, all living – will be judged.

Paul reminds his readers that they are God's building project (3:9–17) and that any leader, be he superapostle or not, is only a servant, a bit player in a much larger drama (3:5–9; 4:1–18). But he challenges the church, and by implication the leaders who opposed him, to sort out its lifestyle. He points out that they seem willing to accept immorality that would make even their pagan neighbours blush (5:1–12; 6:12–20). He is astounded that the church is so divided (and, by implication, its leaders so distrusted) that it is unable to sort out its problems, and takes its disputes to the secular courts (6:1–11).

These are issues that have been drawn to his attention by Chloe's people (1:11), but other matters have been raised by the church in a letter to him. Now he turns to them. First, he deals with marriage. More specifically, he counters the arguments of some in the church that, as a sign of their spirituality, married couples shouldn't have sex. The guiding principle for Paul is that people should remain as they were when they were converted. If you are married, stay married and have normal sexual relations. (There's a suggestion that the church's problems with immorality stemmed from this nonsensical teaching that married people should abstain from sex.) If you are a slave, stay a slave – although if you are offered freedom, don't fight it. If you are single, stay single because you can be more focused on the work of the kingdom without the distractions of home and family.

Chapter 7 is really paving the way for Paul's discussion in chapters 8 – 10 about Christian freedom and decision-making. In an emphasis that is still hugely unpopular today, Paul suggests that Christians are competent to make decisions about their lifestyle for themselves, based on the Scriptures (Christian teaching) and the guidance of the Holy Spirit. No-one needs a busybody leader directing their every footstep. But, he stresses, such decisions should be made with an eye to their effect on our brothers and sisters, because we are members of one another.

In chapter 11 Paul comes to the thorny issues of the Corinthians' chaotic worship, which will occupy his attention until the end of chapter 14. Their over-realized eschatology meant that they had a distorted view of spiritual gifts (which they saw as trophies to be paraded around) and of the Lord's supper (which they treated as an excuse to party to excess). But it also caused them dangerously to disregard social conventions about gender (chapter 11) and intelligibility (chapter 14), and this made their worship seem strange to outsiders. It must have been very strange indeed, given the excesses prevalent in the pagan cults around them! All this put people off the gospel.

One of Paul's fundamental principles was that we should avoid putting stumbling-blocks in the path of unbelievers who want to explore our faith (9:19–23; 14:23–25). After all, the message of Christ crucified is difficult enough already (1:18–25).

Having tried to address the abuse of worship, Paul tackles their distorted eschatology, the root of all their problems. He begins by reminding them of the gospel he taught them and how that gospel was in accordance with both the Scriptures and the teaching of all the other apostles (15:1–11). He then declares that God has raised Christ from the dead (the foundation of our faith) and that Jesus' resurrection points forward to our resurrection, which has not yet occurred (15:12–57). In the meantime, he says, while we live in the overlap between the ages, we need to stay focused on living lives that honour God and point others to Jesus (15:58).

He rounds the letter off by reminding the Corinthians of the great collection he is gathering from the Gentile churches to take to Jerusalem to help the poorer Jewish church (16:1–4), and by telling them of his travel and ministry plans for the coming months.

The agony of ministry

Relations between Paul and the Corinthians got worse. Timothy's visit was a disaster. New teachers arrived, muddying the waters still further. Paul felt his third letter had misfired. Titus was dispatched, and finally brought Paul news that the relationship was restored.

The apostle had been through the wringer. This fractured relationship affected his ministry in other places (2 Corinthians 2:13). It caused him to doubt his calling and question why he did what he did.

2 Corinthians is a heartbreakingly honest and intimate letter. It is passionate, confessional and angry – often in adjoining sentences. It is a hard letter to read, because its emotions are so raw. We do it no justice if we come to it thinking it to be a dispassionate treatise on reconciliation.

Paul is stunningly open with his readers from the outset. He does not pull rank or blind them with theology. He tells them how hurt he has been by their treatment of him (1:12 – 3:6; 10:10). This experience of rejection has forced him back into the arms of God, his only comfort (1:3–11). He poignantly speaks of how his dejection led to a fresh encounter with God, and how, in the midst of pain, he had learned to trust God even more (4:8–10; 6:1 – 7:1).

All through the letter he both rejoices that he has been reconciled to the majority of the church and recoils in bewildered anger from those who still slander and attack him. The great passage about the reconciliation with God we enjoy through Christ (5:11–21) needs to be read as the culmination of a defence of his ministry that begins in 3:1, and as an appeal to those still holding out to be reconciled to him and through him to Christ (5:16–20). The difference between Paul and his opponents is not just a matter of opinion. To oppose Paul is to oppose God by rejecting the true gospel.

Isn't this rather arrogant on Paul's part? No. The argument hinges on what are the characteristics of a true apostle – indeed, a true follower and representative – of Jesus. Paul argues strongly that his sufferings demonstrate that he is walking in the footsteps of the crucified Messiah, and that true spiritual authority is exercised out of a position of apparent weakness (4:1–18; 11:1–32). His opponents boasted of their fantastic spiritual experiences and asserted that this proved they were the real McCoy, whereas Paul was a rather pathetic specimen whose trials demonstrated that he had not learned the secret of walking in victory all the time.

In a breathtaking moment of self-revelation, Paul counters their charge by recalling great experiences he had had that rival any of his opponents'. But the killer blow is that he has moved beyond that to realize that great experiences are not what matters; rather, dependence on God is all that counts, and that is demonstrated not in untouchable strength but in all-too-bloodied weakness (12:1–10).

One of the key contrasts between Paul and his opponents is that he lived his life for others, pouring himself out in the hard graft of ministry on behalf of believer and unbeliever alike. His opponents sought only to feather their own nests; they were desperately inward-looking and self-obsessed. In the midst of his appeal for reconciliation across the board, Paul urges the church to be outward-looking and to recognize that the needs of others had a legitimate call on their lives and resources (8:1 – 9:15). In their generosity, they would be imitating God. In their sacrificial giving, they would be truly following Jesus. And in looking away from themselves to the needs of the wider world, they would gain a sense of perspective and proportion about their problems and what really mattered in the world and the life of faith.

2 Corinthians ought to be compulsory reading for all church members and especially for their leaders, because it reveals the reality of life in the church and charts the way to real encounter with the God of all comfort. It is only in weakness and dependence that we truly meet and walk with the crucified Messiah. This is a theme we will tackle in our next chapter.

Questions

1. What picture of leadership emerges from 1 and 2 Corinthians? Think in particular about how Paul deals with the opposition to his leadership.
2. What is the church's role according to Ephesians? How does your church fulfil this role?
3. What's the place of suffering – opposition, persecution, etc. – in the Christian life?
4. What reasons does Paul give why the church should be outward-looking?
5. What do you think Paul meant by saying that he was all things to all people (1 Corinthians 9)? How do you seek to put this into practice in your life at home, at work and at church?

6

Following Jesus, preparing to meet him

1 and 2 Thessalonians, Philippians

Have you ever wondered where Paul got his energy from – planting churches by day, shooting off letters at night and still able to turn the best tents in town? There's no secret formula, but over the next week as we read this chapter and 1 and 2 Thessalonians and Philippians, we'll learn to live on what Paul lived on. Try reading the three letters right through each day on days 2–5. Alternatively, follow the plan.

Day 1 Read this chapter.
Day 2 Read 1 Thessalonians.
Day 3 Read 2 Thessalonians.
Day 4 Read Philippians.
Day 5 Re-read the letter you knew least well (probably 2 Thessalonians).
Day 6 Re-read this chapter and look at the discussion questions.
Day 7 Meet with the friends you are reading this book with, have a meal or a drink, and talk through the discussion questions and anything else that struck you through your reading.

Christians in the West often have a rather privatized view of their faith. It seems to be about eternal security and personal morality and precious little else. Its focus is an hour or so on a Sunday morning which tends to reinforce the idea that Jesus is only really interested in my soul, my marital fidelity and my not swearing at my workmates.

This is a far cry from the good news Paul proclaimed around the Roman Empire. His gospel was about a king, a rival to Caesar, who demanded the allegiance of the whole world (just as Caesar did). And although this king was not physically present at the moment, he was coming imminently to judge and to rule. Christians who had chosen to obey King Jesus' call to follow and serve him, rather than rival kings and gods, ordered their lives in the light of these two facts.

It meant that discipleship for those early Christians was a 24/7 affair: twenty-four hours a day, seven days a week. Following Jesus was not a religious activity. It was a way of life, affecting work, leisure, politics, home and family. Christian spirituality revolutionized people's relationship with the world. While this truth lurked in the background of all Paul's writing, it is the main theme of letters he wrote to the key Roman cities of Philippi and Thessalonica, where he had planted churches at the opening of the 50s.

Whose side are you on?

These two cities were important centres in the Roman province of Macedonia (now northern Greece). Philippi was a Roman colony and administrative centre for the region, and possibly Luke's home town. Thessalonica was the largest city in the region, a major sea port on the main trade route from Europe to Asia (the *Via Egnatia*), and thus a cosmopolitan place teeming with people of just about every culture of the Empire and beyond.

Both were centres of vibrant local religions and cults. More importantly, both embraced the cult of emperor worship (see chapters 19 and 20) with a gusto not seen in Italy or western Europe. Here Caesar was both *Kyrios* and *Sōtēr*, titles the Christians reserved exclusively for their king, Jesus. When Nero said that he was lord and saviour, he wasn't offering the people of the Empire a religious option on a 'take it or leave it' basis. The offer was, 'Worship me or face the consequences.' In this cultural and spiritual environment, Paul's command to turn from other allegiances and to serve the one true Lord and Saviour, Jesus Christ, rang out through the streets of both these cities. And in both it was met with a mixture of bewilderment and faith, fury and repression.

Paul and his team arrived in Philippi in AD 49 or 50 and began preaching the good news (Acts 16:11–40). He soon ran into trouble with powerful religious and political vested interests, and he and Silas were beaten up and imprisoned. About midnight, their singing caused an earthquake that led to the conversion of the jailer and his family. The following day the magistrates ordered their release. But Paul refused to go quietly, because, as a Roman citizen, he'd been treated illegally. He demanded his rights partly because he wanted to travel the Empire without an unjust criminal record hanging round his neck, and also because he had been treated unjustly and he was not prepared to take it like a doormat.

Apology duly given, Paul and Silas set off and arrived down the road in Thessalonica. It's clear from 1 Thessalonians that they stayed longer than the four weeks implied by Luke's account (Acts 17:1–9). Paul's team, which included Timothy as well as Silas (17:14–15), worked in the port city for some months, making leather goods in a hired workshop, sharing the gospel and establishing a flourishing church among mainly Gentile converts.

Once again, they ran into trouble. Paul was proclaiming a message about a king and urging people to swear allegiance to him. The Thessalonians had only one king: Caesar (Acts 17:7). Serious opposition brewed against the apostles. Prudence suggested that the church should hide the missionaries and spirit them away once darkness fell. In their place, Jason (a wealthy convert) and others were roughed up for their treasonable activities.

Paul moved sixty miles southwest to Berea and then to Athens. Not long after he left Thessalonica, he wrote twice to the church there – probably in the space of just a couple of weeks in 52 or 53. Many years later, when Paul was in prison in Rome, he wrote to the church in Philippi (probably around AD 61). We'll look at these three letters in the order in which they were written, and focus on the key themes of discipleship that emerge from them.

Lives that speak louder than words

The Thessalonian letters are the most overtly apocalyptic texts that Paul wrote. (See chapter 16 for an explanation of what apocalyptic is all about.) It is possible that he had accentuated the apocalyptic elements of his preaching and teaching because it resonated with his Thessalonian audience, in much the same way that in Athens he had constructed his message out of references to local poets, Cynic and Stoic writings and inscriptions because such an approach pushed the right buttons in his hearers (Acts 17:22–33; see chapter 19).

Apart from emperor worship, the Thessalonians' main cult focused on a deity called Cabirius. His image appeared on the coins; his festivals marked out the official calendar. He was a hero from Thessalonica's past who had died defending the city and had been elevated to the pantheon of gods. Adherents believed that on occasion he returned to life and came to the aid of the poor of Thessalonica. The ceremony of initiation into his cult involved being 'baptized' in water as a symbolic immersion in Cabirius' blood.

Clearly, Paul's gospel of a martyred Messiah through whom sins were dealt with and who was coming imminently to judge the world, and particularly to call to account those who had persecuted his followers, would have found a ready hearing in such an environment.

The most obviously apocalyptic feature of the Thessalonian letters is Paul's teaching on the second coming of Christ. Nowhere else does Paul devote so much space to this subject, which suggests that it was a pressing concern for the Thessalonian Christians. But Paul's teaching about Christian lifestyle is also set in the framework of the tension of the 'now' and the 'not yet' so characteristic of Christian apocalyptic.

1 Thessalonians 1:9–10 is a summary of Paul's original preaching in the city. It makes no reference to Old Testament promises. Paul was seeking to communicate his gospel in language that his predominantly Gentile hearers would be able to make sense of and respond to. And respond they did. Paul positively glows with pride at how these young Christians took his message to heart and became examples to other churches way beyond their city walls (1:4–11).

Two themes dominate the rest of the letter, and both shed shafts of light on what it means to be a disciple of Jesus.

The first is Paul's relationship with the church. It's possible that Paul is writing to defend himself against criticism from people who have arrived in the church since his departure. But this is unlikely. It's too soon for new teachers to have got a toe-hold in this community. It's more likely that Paul is reminding them of how their community came into being and thus what are the distinguishing marks of their Christian identity: they were to be like Paul and his team in both their personal and their communal lives.

Paul isn't boasting. He's just telling it like it was. He, Silas and Timothy set up shop, worked for a living and shared their faith as a natural part of their daily conversation (2:1–16). As the number of converts grew, the apostles cared for them like a mother (2:7) and father (2:11) combined. The converts responded to a message that they not only heard but saw with their eyes and experienced in the way Paul and his team dealt with them. The point that Paul is trying to make is that they should behave in the same way (2:13–16).

But if they lived this way they would suffer – as they were already finding out (1:6; 2:13–16). They lived in the agonizing tension of the 'now' and the 'not yet' of the Christian faith. Now they had been saved by faith in Christ and filled with the Holy Spirit. But they had not yet received freedom from the burdens of this life or the persecutions of those opposed to God and his king, Jesus. They eagerly awaited the coming of Jesus with its promise of release from pain into joyous fulfilment of their hope (1:10; 5:9–10).

And perhaps they were getting restless. Paul was clearly concerned for them. Because he longed to see them, he dispatched Timothy to find out how they were doing, and rejoiced at the encouraging news his friend brought back (2:17 – 3:13). Perhaps Paul feared that because he'd had to leave so suddenly, the infant believers would struggle because he hadn't been able to complete his teaching programme with them (3:10). He needn't have worried. Timothy's report confirmed that the Holy Spirit was able to complete what Paul had failed to finish (3:12–13).

Time running out?

But there was one area of concern: the return of King Jesus. It seems that some Thessalonian believers had died, perhaps at the hands of their persecutors. How long would this go on? When would Jesus show up to free them from op-pression, as Cabirius had allegedly done for their ancestors? Paul needed to correct some misunderstandings about Christian hope, which is the second main theme of the letter.

Some commentators suggest that the very early Christians believed that Jesus would return within (at the most) a generation of his resurrection. Slowly over time, this hope faded and the church settled down to business as usual on earth. This is nonsense. The early Christians believed firmly in the second coming of Jesus, but, from the earliest days of the new movement, they had no idea when it would be. So they lived their daily lives doing all the things you need to do to get through the day in the light of that event. Perhaps the hope of Jesus' return has faded for some commentators and they project their insecurities back on the early church.

The Thessalonians were a special case, perhaps because of their particular pagan background. But what Paul said to them applies to us all. The Christian hope is that those who die having put their faith in Jesus will be raised when Jesus comes again (4:13 – 5:11). So we don't grieve as those without hope – though we do grieve because we feel the loss of loved ones acutely, even though we know we shall see them again. We don't know when the second coming will happen (5:1–3), but we know it *will* happen, because Jesus has been raised from the dead (5:9–10). So we need to be alert to his return and live each day accordingly (5:4–8, 11).

Now this should have satisfied his readers, but it didn't. So much is clear from 2 Thessalonians. Indeed, it's possible that Paul's words here added to the Thessalonians' anxiety. After getting 1 Thessalonians, the church had received another letter allegedly from Paul or his circle, claiming that the day of the Lord had already dawned (2 Thessalonians 2:1–2). This worried them even more. In the most apocalyptic passage in any of his writing, Paul therefore assures his readers that certain general things have to happen before the second coming, and they haven't happened yet (2:3–12). Libraries have been filled with detailed timetables explaining what Paul meant in these verses. Few of these books are good for anything but bonfires.

Paul's intention was not to provide a countdown to the second coming so that we could sit back with a checklist and reassure ourselves that it won't be happening this week. Neither was it his intention to scare the wits out of his already vulnerable readers. Rather, he wrote to correct a narrowness in the Thessalonians' vision. They seemed to assume that God's plans revolved around them. They were suffering terribly, so this must be a sign that the Day was about to dawn. Not so, says Paul. This suffering is a little local difficulty; things will get worse before they get better all over the world.

His aim is not to provoke speculation about who the 'lawless one' is (2:3), or who 'the one who now restrains it' is (2:7). Rather, the very vagueness of Paul's language seems to be urging us not to lose the plot by believing that every negative event is a sign of the imminent end of all things. This attitude was leading people to give up the normal daily routine of work and family life to wait in apocalyptic ardour for the coming of the king (2 Thessalonians 3:6–14). Part of our difficulty is that Paul is summarizing teaching he gave much more fully when he was in Thessalonica (2:5). There's more information on this difficult passage in *Discovering 1 and 2 Thessalonians* (pages 145–159).

Paul's point in both letters is to reassure his readers that Jesus is coming again, and that one day they will enjoy life in his kingdom without persecution or pain. But now the focus is on living in the present in the light of that coming event. Hence, he says, they should keep themselves from sexual immorality (1 Thessalonians 4:1–8), they should care for and support one another (4:9–10) and they should live exemplary lives in the community (4:11).

Some have suggested that this verse is telling the Thessalonians to have nothing to do with public or political life. In fact, Paul seems to be urging his readers to do the opposite. The words recall Paul's example, of which he has already reminded them (2:1–12). Paul and his colleagues lived their lives in public. They worked and traded, and their workshop no doubt became a hub of business and discussion. Through this, many of his readers had come to faith in Christ. Paul is now keen that others in Thessalonica should see and hear the gospel through the lives and words of his readers. This is vital in view of the all-too-real fate awaiting those who don't bow the knee to King Jesus willingly now (2 Thessalonians 1:5–10).

So Paul constantly calls his readers to their 'work'. He thanked God that their faith was seen in work (1 Thessalonians 1:3), he reminds them of his example of work (2:9), calls them to follow it (4:11), and urges them to honour those who work among them in teaching them their faith (5:13). Furthermore, he prays that God will inspire every good work in them (2 Thessalonians 1:11; 2:17), that each believer will work as he or she is able (3:10–11) and that we will never tire of doing what is right (3:13); in this we will be following Paul's example (3:8).

What we notice about all these references is that Paul moves seamlessly between what we would label 'secular' and 'sacred'. His message is simple: everything we do, we do for God; discipleship is a 24/7 activity. And the purpose of this? That others may see and hear the good news of Jesus and bow the knee to him as king before he comes again and forces everyone to bow to him.

Following in the Master's footsteps

For Paul, Christian living was fired by the hope of God's coming kingdom. He had been raised on a diet of apocalyptic writing (see chapter 16), which taught him that at the end of this current age of sin, violence and injustice, a new age of peace, justice and God's perfect rule would dawn. These hopes had found their focus in Jesus, who dragged the new age of the kingdom into the current age, so that his followers lived in a time of overlap between these two ages.

Philippians positively bristles with the tension of the 'now' and the 'not yet' of the Christian life. It is in such tension that our discipleship has to be lived out.

Following Paul's departure from Philippi, it's clear that the Judaizers, who bedevilled his ministry throughout the eastern Empire, had got their fangs into this young church. His letter to them is often described as one of joy, and there is much joy in it. But there is also fierce and dismissive anger directed at those who would force Gentiles to follow Jewish practices (3:2).

But instead of taking his enemies on head to head (as he had done in Galatians), he urges the Philippians to imitate his way of being of Christian rather than that of his opponents. Philippians is Paul's most personal letter. For although there's more about Paul's life in 2 Corinthians, in Philippians Paul uses his autobiography to lay out for these young believers a pattern of life lived in the tension of the 'now' and the 'not yet' of Christian eschatology.

Having told the Philippians how he is praying for them (1:3–11), he draws their attention to his plight as a prisoner (1:12–30). But instead of bemoaning his lot, he assures them that what has happened to him has advanced the cause of the gospel and that this is a reason for rejoicing. It's important to realize that Paul is probably under house arrest at this time and thus unable to continue his public ministry, which is indeed part of his legal defence against the charges brought against him. The language he uses in this section of the letter is the language people used of political and legal affairs. He is stressing that his conduct is the same in court as it is in church. And he urges his readers to live in the world in the same way (1:27–30 – the word translated 'live your life', *politeuesthe*, actually means 'live as citizens' and belongs to the word-group from which we get 'politics'). They will be opposed just as Paul has been; they will be persecuted just as Paul has been. Whatever happens to them, they are to meet it as Paul has done.

The reason for this is that we follow a Master who similarly suffered and left us an example of how to meet opposition and persecution. We should be guided by the same attitude that guided Jesus, says Paul (2:5). Then he produces one of the most sublime portraits of our Lord anywhere in the New Testament. Whether he composed this at the time of writing or used a passage that he'd used many times before in worship, this poem is full of Pauline language and was almost certainly written by him at some time in his ministry. It tells us clearly that Jesus was God and that God's character is seen in his life, which was marked by humility and servanthood (2:6–11). This is the pattern of life we should adopt (2:12–18).

Then, having brought his readers up to speed on his team's travel plans, Paul launches into the most intimate autobiographical passage in any of his letters. His focus is still on how the Philippians should live in the world, but he has now turned his attention to those who would lead them astray. Having angrily denounced them (3:1–3), he gives us his testimony of what it means for him to walk as Jesus did (3:4–14). He is the pharisaic Jew who met Jesus, and who through that encounter stopped trying to impose Jewish ways on the world. Now he is consumed by a desire to know Jesus. Here is a Paul who hasn't got it all, but is pressing on towards the goal of knowing Jesus better and eventually being where he is. This is the 'now' and the 'not yet' of Christian apocalyptic agonizingly working itself out in Paul's life (cf. 2:12–13). Again he urges his readers to follow him in this (3:15 – 4:1).

Finally, he turns his attention to discipleship in the church. It is clear from Philippians that there was no such thing as a lone Christian in Paul's book (see 2:1–5, where all the 'you's' are plural). We are in this adventure of faith together. God's intention is to call a single, united people out of all the nations of the earth.

Because of this, he pleads with two Philippian leaders to agree with each other. Philippians 3:1 – 4:4 seems to form what is called an *inclusio* – a passage that begins and ends with the same thought (in this case, Paul urging the Philippians to rejoice) and thus has a single theme. What he is saying is that together we need to press on towards the things that matter, so the things that Euodia and Syntyche have fallen out over really aren't all that important in the light of the goal we're all aiming for. It's likely that one of these two female leaders of the church has bought into the Judaizers' line and the other hasn't, and now they are slogging it out in public. Paul urges them to agree with each other that what matters is that we press on together towards the goal he has shown us, rather than fall out over trivial details.

Having thanked the church for providing support for him while he was in Thessalonica – tangible proof of their fellowship in the gospel and their need for each other as they seek to live for Jesus in a hostile world – Paul signs off with a warm greeting, not only from him but from everyone sharing his ministry and sufferings in Rome.

Eyes on the prize

For Paul, to know Christ is to know God and to be caught up in his kingdom. Thus, living and dying, health and suffering, enjoying peace or enduring persecution all pale into insignificance beside the joy of this knowledge (1:21).

But this knowledge isn't merely an intellectual exercise. It is about our lifestyle. The two key passages of the letter are

2:6–11 and 3:4–14: Paul wants to follow and know the Christ he has described in chapter 2. This is the Jesus who met him on the road to Damascus, who called him to be a minister to the Gentiles; this is the Jesus who knows him intimately and whom Paul is desperate to know. He is on a journey of discovery, and in order to make that journey, he has resolved to lose all the things he used to think important – his culture, his old beliefs, his old way of life (3:4–8). He decided to do this because the Jesus he'd met on the road to Damascus wanted to know Paul despite his bigotry and blindness. And now Paul wants to know him. On that occasion Jesus had been a booming voice and blinding light, a powerful, mysterious and intriguing presence. Paul's life since that encounter had been the search for an answer to the question, 'Who are you, Lord?' (Acts 9:5).

In particular, Paul wants his life to be marked by the resurrection (3:10). For the resurrection has changed the rules of living. Now it is possible to live as God wants us to. We need not be bound by our genes, our culture, our sins, our screw-ups. We can be freed from these things through the power of Jesus' resurrection. And we can know that power only by walking the way of the cross.

Ah, there's the rub: there is no resurrection without a cross. Paul is in prison, and his life has been marked by suffering and hardship. Discipleship is not a soft option. It is not a Sunday-morning alternative to washing the car.

Paul urges the Philippians to live in the same way. Whether it's at home or at work, in the private sphere or the political arena, we are to live in such a way that people see something of the life of Christ in us. This is what it means to shine as stars in the midst of a crooked and depraved generation (2:15). Jesus isn't just interested in our souls. He wants our lives. Discipleship, says Paul, is about what we do and say twenty-four hours a day, seven days a week, whether we're in church or at work, down the pub or in Parliament. In all that we do, we hold out the word of life (2:16) in order that when King Jesus comes to judge and to reign, many may welcome him as a result of how we have lived in this world.

Questions

1. What does it mean to live each day in the light of Jesus' second coming? What hints are there in 1 and 2 Thessalonians that might help us to do this?
2. Look at all the references to 'work' and 'doing' in the Thessalonian letters. What does this tell us about how we live in the church? At home? In the world?
3. What are the things we should be counting as loss for the surpassing worth of knowing Jesus? (Clues in Philippians 3:1–15.)
4. Do we know the Jesus Paul describes in Philippians 2:6–11? How can we model our lives on this Jesus and reflect him to those around us?
5. Look up all the references in Philippians to 'joy' and 'rejoicing'. How do they speak to you? Do they give you a message for someone you know? (There's a note on this in *Discovering Philippians*, pages 125–126.)

Let's get personal

Philemon, 1 and 2 Timothy, Titus

Having a bad time with colleagues at work? Wish you'd written to say 'thanks' for the help a friend gave when it was really needed? Want to know what to write to encourage a missionary? Over the next six days, as we read this chapter and Philemon, 1 Timothy, Titus and 2 Timothy, we'll come away with all sorts of hints about building relationships. As usual, you can either follow the plan below or read all the texts being studied right through each day on days 2–5.

Day 1 Read this chapter.
Day 2 Read Philemon.
Day 3 Read 1 Timothy.
Day 4 Read Titus.
Day 5 Read 2 Timothy.
Day 6 Re-read this chapter and look at the discussion questions.
Day 7 Meet with the friends you are reading this book with, have a meal or a drink, and talk through the discussion questions and anything else that struck you through your reading.

We know Paul mainly as a writer of letters to churches. Because of his passion for Christ and devotion to the people in the congregations he'd planted around the Mediterranean world, he wrote letters commending their faithfulness, correcting their errors and generally encouraging them to stick to Jesus like glue.

Paul was very much a team player, always surrounded by a group of fellow-workers who shared the task of church-planting and pastoring, many of them travelling with him across the Roman Empire, sharing his agonies and setbacks as well as his joys and triumphs.

In the midst of his busy life, he found time to write to some of these people. These letters reveal a side of Paul often obscured when we think of him as the fierce defender of truth and corrector of wayward behaviour. They reveal a tender Paul, a pastor who cared deeply for each member of his team; they reveal a man who needed his friends around in times of difficulty – which were many.

We have four of his personal letters in our New Testament: the so-called pastoral letters (1 and 2 Timothy and Titus) and Philemon. All the guys to whom they were addressed were in some way involved in Christian ministry and church leadership. Timothy was a frequent travelling companion of Paul's, a trusted lieutenant, to whom he gave the responsibility of leading the church at Ephesus in the 60s. Titus likewise led the church on Crete, having also travelled with Paul. Philemon was a leader of a house church in Colosse.

Bringing people together

The letter to Philemon was written at the same time as, and sent along with, the letter to the Colossians. It's 60 or 61, and Paul is under house arrest in Rome, having appealed to Caesar months earlier when in Jerusalem (see chapter 21). Although awaiting trial, he is able to preach, teach and catch up with his correspondence. As he pens a letter to Colosse giving advice on how they can resist the false teachers troubling the church, he decides to send a short letter to his old friend Philemon, converted under his ministry in Ephesus, and now leader of a house church in the Lycus valley between Colosse and Laodicea.

The reason for this is simple. Paul has got something of Philemon's. Since he has been in prison, a runaway slave called Onesimus has pitched up – whether looking for Paul or accidentally coming across him, we don't know – and has become a Christian. Having been reconciled to God through Jesus, Onesimus now needed to be reconciled to his master. Paul had taught about this often enough (see especially 2 Corinthians 5:16–21). So he writes a letter and sends Onesimus back with it. Paul hoped not only that Philemon and his slave would be reconciled, but that the master would treat his slave as his equal and grant him his freedom (verse 16). There's even a possibility that Paul is suggesting to Philemon that he should send Onesimus back to Rome to work with Paul, because the apostle has found him to be very useful indeed (a play on Onesimus' name, which means 'useful' in Greek; see verses 10–11).

But this letter is about more than restoring a runaway slave to his master. In its simple, disarming way, it is a lovely treatise on the value of Christian relationships and how to restore them when they break down. Indeed, it is an exposition in everyday life of the truth that we are all one, equal in Christ. The key to understanding the letter is verses 4–7, Paul's prayer about Philemon's character and especially his love.

Paul commends Philemon's faith in Jesus and love for the saints (verse 5). It is probable that Paul meant both 'faith' (best understood as 'loyalty' or 'faithfulness') and 'love' to apply to both 'Jesus' and the 'saints', so that the verse reads, 'I hear about your loyalty to and love for the Lord Jesus and all the saints.' This is then spelt out in Philemon's active sharing – the word is *koinōnia* – of his life with those around him, something that Paul himself has experienced (verse 7). The thrust of these verses is that faith in Jesus leads us to have a practical, sharing love with all his people, for they are our family. Philemon, a man of some wealth, was generous in sharing all he had with those around him in the church. This, according to Paul, is what normal Christian living is all about.

When relationships in the church (which should marked

by openness, sharing, generosity and fellowship) break down, something needs to be done pretty quickly to put them right. Philemon's relationship with Onesimus has broken down big time. Onesimus had run away, and probably did so taking a quantity of Philemon's goods and cash with him (verse 18). Philemon was entitled to punish him severely, and he would have the full weight of the law on his side if he did so.

But Paul's appeal is born of the fact that our faith in Jesus changes everything, including the way we relate to those 'higher' or 'lower' than us on the social scale. We are all one in Christ (verses 16–17), and that should be seen in generous acceptance of one another, forgiving one another just as God in Christ forgave us. The theology of all this is in 2 Corinthians 5:11–21; Galatians 3:26–28; Ephesians 2:11–22 and Romans 15:7. Here in this lovely little letter we have the appeal of one elderly man to another to ensure that this great theology leads to real actions affecting the lives of real people.

Another fine mess

When we turn to the so-called Pastoral Letters, we see what happens when bad theology is unleashed on the real lives of real people. These letters display Paul's struggles with false teaching and his passionate concern that God's people should live lives that radiate the grace of Christ to those around them.

These letters come from very late in Paul's life. After the end of Acts, when we presume that Paul was released from house arrest in Rome, he came east (possibly having first gone to Spain) planting churches as he came and revisiting some he'd founded a decade or more before. And everywhere he went, it seems, there was trouble or the threat of it.

1 Timothy and Titus were written in response to situations in the churches at Ephesus and on Crete in the mid-60s. Having planted congregations on Crete, Paul and Timothy had moved on, leaving Titus to ensure that the

new churches were properly established. On reaching
Ephesus, the duo encountered the chaos of false teaching,
and Paul left Timothy to sort that situation out while he
moved on. Then, from Macedonia, he wrote to both his
young colleagues encouraging them to stick to the task he'd
left them to do.

It is obvious from the letter that Timothy was having a
torrid time in Ephesus. Usually, when Paul had to counter
false teaching, it came from outsiders who'd come into
churches after Paul had moved on. In Ephesus the false
teachers were insiders, even leaders of some of the house
churches – just as Paul himself had predicted would happen
(Acts 20:30).

Paul tells us three things about these false teachers. First,
it appears that they were influenced by a mixture of Jewish
and pagan ideas and had created a sort of pick-and-mix
faith out of elements that appealed to them. In that respect,
they resembled some parts of today's New Age movement.
Secondly, they seem to have been targeting women,
especially vulnerable, newly widowed, younger women,
which accounts for Paul's uncharacteristic bar on women
teaching in church (2:9–15; 5:3–16; see 2 Timothy 3:6–9 and
the helpful discussion of 1 Timothy 2:11–12 in *Discovering
Timothy and Titus*, pages 55–64). And thirdly, they seem to
have been motivated by one thing and one thing only: cash.
Religion to them was just a way of making a fast drachma
(1:3–7; 6:3–10). These elements make them sound very
contemporary indeed!

Paul writes to his young colleague, urging him to correct
the false teaching and to stand up to the false teachers.
Although the letter is a personal one, written to a specific
individual, it was intended for wider consumption. The
reason Paul didn't write to the church – as he had once
before in his great letter to the Ephesians – was that he
wanted to bolster Timothy's position (1:3–6, 10) against
those opposed to Paul's gospel (1:18–20). By addressing the
letter to Timothy, Paul is saying to the church, 'Here's my
man. Listen to him and you'll not go astray.'

Paul urges Timothy to ensure that 'sound doctrine' is

preached, but he doesn't spell out what that doctrine is. This is for two reasons. The first is that since Timothy is a long-standing colleague of Paul's, Timothy knows full well what the truth is. The second is that he's telling the church that whatever Timothy says is sound doctrine that comes with Paul's stamp of approval – unlike the nonsense being spouted by Hymanaeus, Alexander and the rest (4:1–8, especially verse 6).

In chapters 2 and 3, Paul talks about how church life should be organized, not because he's concerned about ecclesiastical niceties, but because this will ensure good teaching, which is the essential prerequisite for good Christian conduct in the world (3:15 – a key verse in the letter, the theme of which Paul returns to at the end: 6:17–19). Then, in chapters 5 and 6, he focuses on some of the specific problems: namely, the widows who've been led astray, and the powerful evil effects that money can have, even on a Christian. And all the time he's urging Timothy to stand firm in the truth he's known all his life (4:1–15; 5:11–16).

Building on firm foundations

While Timothy was battling with false teachers, Titus was building on the foundations laid by Paul in Crete. He'd been left behind to ensure that the churches they'd founded were organized in such a way that they didn't fall prey to the kind of false teachers plaguing the Ephesian church.

Because they were written at the same time, the letter to Titus shares some of the same concerns as 1 Timothy. But because the circumstances of the two churches differed, in his letter to Titus Paul focused less on false teachers and more on Christian lifestyle.

The church on Crete was still in its infancy. So Paul writes to encourage Titus to do two things. The first is to appoint leaders. He doesn't tell Titus how to appoint them, but he does outline the sort of qualities leaders should have – just as he did to Timothy. One of the key elements is that leaders should know the good news about Jesus and be able to teach others about it, whether by preaching or by running a home group.

Some commentators have argued that Paul couldn't have written the Pastorals because the picture of the church given in these late letters differs so much from the freer, charismatic congregations pictured in 1 Corinthians and other early letters. But this is not necessarily the case. Philippians, an early letter, was written to church members and leaders (Philippians 1:1). The church always had leaders (see Acts 6:1–7; 14:21–24). The fact that Paul stresses to both Timothy and Titus the need for good leaders who can teach should not lead us to the conclusion that the church was becoming institutionalized. What we must guard against is reading later church organization and structures back into the Pastoral Letters and assuming that they give us a picture of a church that is becoming rigidly hierarchical. The very fact that some leaders in Ephesus had gone off the rails and some hadn't, and the very fact that Paul had to install his man, Timothy, and try to bolster his authority by writing him a strongly worded letter, the contents of which he was to share with the whole church, suggest that church life and organization were still pretty loose and free. It suggests that people who claimed to be inspired by the Holy Spirit and to have a 'new' revelation of how things should be done could still get a hearing – to the benefit or detriment of the church, depending on what this new thing was.

The church still consisted of small gatherings of believers (probably no more than thirty in any one congregation) who met in homes across cities, relating loosely to each other but having no centralized controlling leadership (see chapter 23). The leader of one of these small groups was not a pastor in our sense of the word, but someone more like a home-group leader – an ordinary working person with a bit of Christian experience and knowledge, who hosted the congregation and gave a shape to its meetings. These people mattered – and still do. They had a considerable influence over the health of the church. If they got infected by false understandings of the good news, it is likely that those meeting in their home would pick the infection up – like flu going round a home group in winter.

This is why Paul lays such stress on leaders being able to teach and pass on the basics of the Christian faith to their congregations. It is also why he insists that in their lifestyle they model Christian behaviour (Titus 1:5–16). Leaders don't just teach through their words; they also teach through what people see in their lives.

The second item on Paul's agenda to Titus is to remind him what he – and by implication all the leaders he appoints – should teach. The dominant theme of chapters 2 and 3 of this letter is that a Christian's life should be focused on good works (1:8, 16; 2:7, 4; 3:1, 8, 14). Paul stresses that Christian believers should exercise self-control – a favourite theme of his (see 1 Corinthians 8 – 10). This is not spiritualized self-help. Rather, in Paul's view, self-control is a fruit of the Spirit (Galatians 5:22). It is inspired by the Holy Spirit and based on sound Christian teaching. The reason he stresses it in Titus is that it will protect the people in his care from the manipulation that Christians in Ephesus are experiencing from leaders who seek to exercise undue influence over members of their congregations.

But self-control is not an end in itself. Its purpose is to enable Christians to focus on how they should live, both in the church and in the wider world, so that the good news about Jesus is seen and experienced by people (2:5, 7, 8, 10, 11; 3:1, 8). Paul's passion throughout his ministry was that as many people as possible should come to experience and understand the freedom and new life that God brings us in Jesus. That is what Titus should be teaching on Crete. That should be the focus of all our home-group activity.

A final word to a favourite son

This brings us to 2 Timothy, surely one of the most moving letters ever written. Paul is now in prison in Rome. It is late 65 or early 66. Nero's persecution of Christians is hotting up and Paul is about to become yet another of its victims (4:6). And so he writes to Timothy.

People are deserting him. In Ephesus they are abandoning his teaching in favour of something sub-gospel that leaves people in thrall to money-grabbing religious hucksters. Probably the false teachers are able to use Paul's imprisonment as evidence that Paul's gospel is substandard (1:15; 2:16–18; 4:14–15). But even close colleagues, such as Demas (Colossians 4:14), are losing heart, quitting the race and bailing out (4:10a). Others have had to go off to attend to urgent business elsewhere (4:10b, 12), including the ever-trustworthy Titus. Only Luke is with him (4:11a). He's about to stand trial for his life and he needs some support, and the presence of close and trusted friends and colleagues. So he asks Timothy to come to him and bring Mark along (4:11b; cf. 1:4).

This is an intensely personal letter. It talks fondly of Paul and Timothy's early days together (3:10–11; cf. 1:3–5). It reminds Timothy of the rich heritage of Christian teaching he has grown up with (1:5; 3:14–15). And it urges Timothy to remain loyal to his faith in Jesus, to his calling and to his friend Paul (1:6–14; 2:1–13; 3:10 – 4:5). Like Paul, Timothy must stand fast against the false teachers and ensure that Christians and others get a chance to hear the true gospel, the gospel that frees and brings new life (2:14 – 3:9). He must endure suffering because that's part of discipleship (1:8-12). And now Timothy must leave Ephesus and come to Paul's side (4:9, 11, 21). It's as though Paul is saying that for the short time he has left, his need of Timothy is greater than the Ephesians' need of him.

Though death hangs over this letter, however, it is not a gloomy piece of writing. Paul is not broken by his predicament. He remains focused on proclaiming the good news of Jesus by the way he lives as well as by what he says – and, if needs be, by the way he dies. So the letter is suffused with the glow of a firm and confident faith.

Paul is confident in the message he proclaims (1:8–12; 2:9) and in what that message is based on (3:14–16). He is confident that beyond the grave lies a new and wonderful resurrection life (1:10b, 12; 2:11–13; 4:7–8). But above all he is confident in Christ, who is the source of grace and salvation (1:2, 9b–10; 2:1), the pattern for the life of discipleship Paul and Timothy are living (2:8–13); and also the one to whom Paul and everyone else will give account (4:1, 8). He is also supremely confident that, whatever happens, Jesus will be at his side upholding and strengthening him (1:12; 4:17–18).

It's in the light of all this that Paul speaks about how important his friends are. While others desert him, Onesiphorus showed the kind of friendship in the gospel that Philemon was famous for (1:16–18). (The word used is *koinōnia*, which means participating in something, sharing fully; i.e. 'fellowship'.) While others have to be away on kingdom business, Paul knows that he cannot face this final test utterly alone, and so he calls for Timothy and Mark to join Luke at his side. Why? Well, perhaps he has a few final things to pass on to these trusted colleagues. He wants Timothy to bring the parchment notebooks that he left at Troas (4:13); perhaps those books and scrolls will enable the quartet to study the Bible together. But it is mainly because all through his life Paul has recognized and taught that the Christian life is not lived in isolation. We cannot survive in a harsh and hostile world without the support, comfort and admonition of brothers and sisters; we cannot boldly stand up for our Lord without the help and prayers of those close to us.

At the end of his life, the apostle who has taught this truth models it for his closest friends and for all who read this letter.

Questions

1. Read Philemon 4–7. In what sense is our church or our home group like a family to us?
2. What kind of false teaching would Paul be likely to warn us about in the western church in the twenty-first century?
3. What criteria do we use for choosing leaders, whether pastors, deacons, PCC members, Sunday-school teachers, youth workers or home group leaders? How do these

criteria compare with those in 1 Timothy 3:1–13 and Titus 1:5–16?
4. How do we combat the love of money in our lives?
5. Have you ever attended a teaching course on 'How to prepare for death'? Why not? What do you think Paul would put into such a course, if he were teaching it?

From the shadows to the reality

Hebrews

Sometimes we get stuck in a rut. Our faith follows a comfortable routine and frankly becomes a little dull. We need a fresh perspective, a new angle. And where better to get it than here? Over the next six days we'll read this chapter and Hebrews and refresh our love for Jesus. Try to read Hebrews right through each day on days 2–5. Or you can follow the plan.

Day 1 Read this chapter.
Day 2 Read Hebrews 1 – 3.
Day 3 Read Hebrews 4 – 6.
Day 4 Read Hebrews 7 – 10.
Day 5 Read Hebrews 11 – 13.
Day 6 Re-read this chapter and look at the discussion questions.
Day 7 Meet with the friends you are reading this book with, have a meal or a drink, and talk through the discussion questions and anything else that struck you through your reading.

For years, the BBC has broadcast a twice-weekly radio programme giving its reporters from around the world the chance to bring us news and impressions not normally included in the main bulletins. *From Our Own Correspondent* is refreshing and informative. It shows us that important things are happening outside the capitals of the rich nations. It highlights events that are not focused on the politicians and power-brokers. It rounds out our picture of the world.

When we read the New Testament, our attention is often so concentrated on Paul's letters and the Gospels that we miss the news from other correspondents who bring fresh insights and new light to bear on the Christian landscape. The New Testament rounds out our picture of the Christian world by including writings from James (see chapter 9), Peter and Jude (see chapter 10), John (see chapters 11 and 12) and the author of Hebrews. Each of these is a unique, perceptive voice from the front line, and they deserve more of a hearing than they seem to get in our churches these days. Our intention in this chapter and the next four is to pick out the distinctive things that each of these writers contributes to our understanding of the Christian faith.

Our man in heaven

Hebrews is an odd, even an off-putting, piece of writing. It's awash with talk of angels, long, explicit descriptions of animal sacrifice, details about the tabernacle that Israel used while wandering in the desert, some odd bod called Melchizedek, and a whole load of other stuff that doesn't enter the 'Top One Hundred' list of things that grab the attention of twenty-first-century Christians. At the same time the letter contains some well-known and popular verses. '[The Son] is the reflection of God's glory and the exact imprint of God's very being' (1:3). 'Because he himself was tested by what he suffered, he is able to help those who are being tested' (2:18). 'Let us therefore approach the throne of grace with boldness so that we may receive mercy and find grace to help in time of need' (4:16). 'Therefore, since we are surrounded by so great a cloud of witnesses, let us lay aside every weight and the sin that clings so closely, and let us run with perseverance the race that is set before us, looking to Jesus, the pioneer and perfecter of our faith …' (12:1–2a). 'Jesus Christ is the same yesterday, today and for ever' (13:8). But these few wonderful texts that have ended up on countless fridge magnets and bookmarks have failed to ensure that the rest of the letter gets read.

This is a pity, because as well as being one of the most elegantly written parts of the New Testament, Hebrews brings us a vital and unique portrait of the founder of our faith, the Lord whom we Christians follow and the person the author of this letter describes (in the words of one commentator) as 'our man in heaven'.

Clearing the ground

As with every other part of the New Testament, if we want to understand Hebrews fully, we need to ask and answer certain basic questions. Who wrote it? Who were its first readers? Where did they live? What were their circumstances that gave rise to this letter?

Sadly, we have no idea who the author of this majestic piece of writing was. There has, of course, been no end of speculation as to who penned it. The translators of the King James Bible thought it was Paul. But it certainly wasn't. The author knew some of Paul's circle (13:23 refers to Timothy – almost certainly the same Timothy who was a colleague of Paul's), but the style, language and way of writing are so unlike Paul's that it cannot have come from the same pen as Romans, 1 Corinthians and the rest.

Other suggestions include Barnabas, Philip, Apollos, Priscilla (and Aquilla), Luke, Silas, Peter, Jude, Clement of Alexandria, Stephen, Aristion and Epaphras. Indeed, a case has been made for just about anyone mentioned in the New Testament being the author of Hebrews. One scholar even suggested, somewhat bizarrely, that Mary the mother of Jesus wrote it!

All we can say for sure about the author is that he (it almost certainly was a 'he') knew his Old Testament inside out (and was thus a Jewish Christian) and that he wrote wonderful, stylish Greek prose, suggesting that he was a highly educated Jew living away from Israel (part of what was known as the Jewish Diaspora, which simply means 'dispersion'). So maybe, out of the list of names above, Silas,

Apollos and Barnabas are the closest fit.

We can be more certain that the original readers of Hebrews were Jewish believers. It is inconceivable that a letter which makes such detailed reference to the Old Testament and expects such a high level of familiarity with the Hebrew Scriptures could have been sent to a congregation of Gentile Christians. There may have been Gentiles among its original recipients; there were few Jewish-only congregations by the time this letter was written. But the majority of its first readers were Jewish. Perhaps the letter was not intended for all the members of a particular congregation, but only for a Jewish section within it – a section that was well known to the author.

Furthermore, they were people who'd been Christians for quite a while. Several references within the letter bear this out. For instance, some of the readers appear to have been in danger of 'drifting' from their faith (2:1–4); some were losing the boldness of profession they once had (3:6–11; 10:35–39); some, maybe, were in danger of committing apostasy (3:12–19; 6:6; 10:29). There's evidence that, having started well, they are not progressing in their faith, but are constantly wanting to go over the basics again and again (5:11–14). There's also clear evidence that in the face of outside pressure (whether outright persecution or pressure from non-Christian family members who were still worshippers at the synagogue) they were contemplating giving up their faith because it didn't seem to be working any more (10:26–39; 12:2–11).

At the root of all these difficulties, it seems that these people were unsure about who Jesus was and is. It seems that because Jesus had not returned, they were wondering whether *anything* they had been told about him was true (2:1–4). And because of that, their faith was increasingly unsatisfying and shaky.

Feeling the pinch

Part of the problems faced by these first readers undoubtedly resulted from their location. They were feeling the pinch of outside interference. People were putting pressure on them because of their ethnicity and their faith in Jesus. Their ethnicity marked them out as a recognizable community in the city they lived in. Their faith in Jesus cut them off from other members of that community.

Although a number of cities would fit the bill, it is most likely that the first readers lived in Rome and were members of one of the small house churches that had sprung up all over that city by the mid-40s. This is confirmed by the reference in 10:32–34 to circumstances that fit very well with the expulsion of Jews from Rome by Claudius in AD 49.

The writer is clearly looking back to this event, which is referred to in Acts 18:2. What seems to have happened is that disputes arose in the Jewish community over the preaching of Christ. The Roman historian Suetonius tells us that Jews at this time were making disturbance at the instigation of one 'Chrestus' (a misheard reference to 'Christus', i.e. Christ). This evidently led to unrest on such a scale that the Roman authorities, keen to suppress foreign religions and encourage their own cults (see chapters 19 and 20), expelled a large number of Jews. It's not clear whether this was just Jewish Christians or Jews more generally (the latter is more likely). Once the furore died down following Claudius' death, many of the Jews slipped back into the city. Among them were a number of Jewish Christians, and they picked up where they left off.

The writer seems to be mentioning this because another wave of trouble is hitting the Christians. But whereas in AD 49 these readers had cheerfully shouldered the consequences of their faith in Christ, this new burst of opposition was the final straw to a group who had begun to doubt whether being Christians was worthwhile at all, given all the hassle it seemed to attract.

This suggests that Hebrews was written as a pastoral letter – it actually seems to be a sermon or homily with some personal greetings attached to the end – addressed to a small group of Jewish Christians in one of the Roman house churches by a fellow Hebrew believer to encourage them to stand fast in the teeth of Nero's persecution in the mid-60s.

The question is: what could he possibly say that would make a difference?

A breathtaking portrait

At the turn of the third Christian millennium the National Gallery in London ran an exhibition called *Seeing Salvation*. It was a look at aspects of Christian art over the centuries that brought together some exceptional paintings and sculptures. I'd seen quite a few of these works before, and others left me cold. But two pictures in particular caught my attention.

One was Salvador Dali's *Christ of St John of the Cross*, a heaven's-eye view of the crucifixion. I've known and loved this painting since the 1970s, but this was the first time I had seen the original. Its sheer size caused me to see it again, as it were, for the first time.

The other was *Christ Carrying the Cross* by Stanley Spencer. This is a portrait of Good Friday as though it happened in Cookham in Berkshire, and shows Christ with his cross surrounded by ordinary working people going about their ordinary daily work. Spencer's intention had been to convey the sense that everyone in the picture was going about their business. Christ was 'not doing *a* job or *his* job but *the* job', said the artist.

I'd never seen this painting before and I stood in front of it gobsmacked. It took my breath away. The simplicity of the figures, the ordinariness of the scene, the sense that everyone is doing what they are meant to do, showed me afresh the wonder of the cross: that Jesus came to do the job of reconciling God and people. I stood silently before the picture for a full five minutes before turning to my companion and mouthing, 'Wow!'

Spencer achieved for me what the writer to the Hebrews hoped to achieve for his first readers. He gave them an utterly breathtaking portrait of Jesus that was intended both to comfort and to challenge them and to help them to see afresh, as though for the first time, the wonder and beauty of their Lord and Saviour.

In chapters 1 – 2 he shows us Jesus as God's Son, so much bigger, brighter and better than the angels; a figure who is undoubtedly divine (1:3) but also utterly human (2:9, 14–18). He was human when he walked the earth and he is human still – the man Jesus enthroned at the right hand of God. He came where we are so that we may be where he is.

In chapters 3 – 4, he gives us Jesus as the true Joshua (the name 'Jesus' is the Greek form of the Hebrew 'Joshua'), leading his people to the promised land – a picture of Jesus as *the* leader, the one to follow to the ends of the earth and beyond, the one to entrust our present and future to. In chapters 5 – 7, Jesus is pictured as the true high priest who makes intercession (7:25). But Jesus is not a priest like the descendants of Aaron, who presided over the daily temple ritual that had to be repeated in perpetuity to ensure the forgiveness of sins. Rather, Jesus is a priest after the order of Melchizedeck, the king of Salem (i:e. Jerusalem) who blessed Abraham (Genesis 14:17–20), the founding father of Israel, and whose priesthood was later understood to be eternal (Psalm 110). But more than that, in chapters 8 – 10, the writer tells us that Jesus is not only the priest, but also the sacrifice whose blood inaugurates a new covenant between God and people.

Then, in chapter 11, he gives us a long list of heroes, great men and women from Israel's past who are examples of faith and courage, who pressed on with God in the hope of one day reaching the heavenly city. And who does this list end with? Who is the greatest of the heroes, even greater than Abraham, Moses and all the prophets? Jesus (12:1–3).

In chapter 13, the writer encourages his readers to stay loyal to this Jesus who remains loyal to them, and who is the same now as he was when they first believed (13:8).

The unfinished story

By any standards, this is a breathtaking portrait. But in order to reinforce his point to his Jewish-Christian audience, this brilliant writer has constructed his portrait out of four key Old Testament passages in order to show his readers how Jesus fulfils and completes that unfinished story.

Chapters 1 – 2 contain reflections on the Psalms and especially Psalm 8. Angels were important figures in the first-century Jewish understanding of God's dealings with his people. They had been particularly involved in the making of the covenant with Moses. They were glorious beings, but Jesus, God's Son, was more glorious, having a more powerful name and a more exalted place than any angel. The Old Testament also suggested that though angels were important, they weren't as important as the human race in God's original plans. Humans were meant to rule the world as God's vice-regents. But they'd blown it because of their sin. The writer of Hebrews picks up Psalm 8's picture of people ruling over God's creation and applies it to Jesus (2:9–18). He is the only human who is living up to God's calling and bringing all things under his feet.

Chapters 3 – 4 pick up the Old Testament promise of entering the land and enjoying the rest that God had promised. The writer's text is Psalm 95:7–11, a great pilgrimage psalm. Although Israel had been in and out of the land for a good millennium by this time (though they were about to be expelled for the best part of the next two millennia), they were not enjoying the level of rest – what the Old Testament described by the Hebrew word *shalom* – that the prophets had spoken of. The writer is saying that Christians are beginning to experience this *shalom* now as a foretaste of what they'll enjoy when Jesus comes again in glory.

Chapters 5 – 7 are a prolonged meditation on Psalm 110. The Old Testament had spoken of a king who was a priest. Yet the kingly line (the house of David) and the priestly line (the house of Aaron) were separate. Jesus was descended from the royal line. But the Old Testament spoke of the Messiah in priestly as well as kingly terms. Psalm 110 (a crucial text in the early church, cropping up in the Gospels, Acts and Paul as well as here in Hebrews), indicates that this will happen. The writer says it has happened in Jesus.

Finally, chapters 8 – 10 pick up Jeremiah's promise of the new covenant (Jeremiah 31:31–34). Having reminded his readers that the old covenant has no permanent solution to the problem of sin, because of the sinfulness of the priests who conduct the rituals at its heart, our author now goes on to show how Jesus, through shedding his own blood on the cross, ushers in the new covenant that Jeremiah foresaw.

All through this wonderful Bible study, the writer's intention is evident. His readers believed the Old Testament; they'd been brought up on it. It was mother's milk to them; it was the source of their identity. Now, he says, its unfinished story was being completed by, in and through Christ.

Staying on the road

The message is clear: don't give up on Jesus. Having painted this breathtaking portrait of their Lord, the author of Hebrews draws three interwoven conclusions that he wants his readers to take away from his homily.

First, woven through his text are countless references to journeys, pilgrimages and following where others have gone before (3 – 4; 11; 12:1–3; 13:13). The writer is reminding his readers that they are on a journey of faith, a journey that is not a Sunday-afternoon meander but a trek through sometimes difficult terrain to a wonderful destination. There might be persecution in store for them, or other difficulties. But these need to be seen against the perspective of the journey as a whole, and of the portrait of the one who calls them to, and leads them through, this journey: namely, Jesus.

Secondly, he is addressing people who are not making this journey alone: they travel in company with others. So he urges and pleads with them to encourage one another (10:23–25) and live in a way that marks their community as one based on the teaching and example of Jesus (13:1–16).

Thirdly, he calls his readers to be outward-looking. There was a danger that this beleaguered little group might remain Christian but lose all confidence in their faith; that they might end up huddled away in the corner as the storm breaks, hoping that no-one would notice them there. The point of continuing to meet together was that they would draw strength from their corporate worship of God and mutual encouragement to live boldly in the world, sharing with those in need and declaring the praises of their Lord to anyone who would listen (13:15–16).

Questions

1. Take the well-known texts mentioned at the start of this study (1:3; 2:18; 4:16; 12:1–2a; 13:8) and produce your own portrait of Jesus.
2. What does Hebrews tell us about how Christians should read and use the Old Testament?
3. How would you draw a portrait of Jesus to rekindle the flagging faith of a fellow-believer?

9

A word from Jerusalem

James

We're meant to be the salt of the earth, but often we feel we must be pretty tasteless people to be with. We see things happening and we wish we had the words to say. We need a good dose of James. Over the next six days we'll read this chapter and James's letter. You can either follow the plan below or read James right through each day on days 2–5.

Day 1 Read this chapter.
Day 2 Read James 1.
Day 3 Read James 2.
Day 4 Read James 3.
Day 5 Read James 4 – 5.
Day 6 Re-read this chapter and look at the discussion questions.
Day 7 Meet with the friends you are reading this book with, have a meal or a drink, and talk through the discussion questions and anything else that struck you through your reading.

Ever since the great Reformer Martin Luther wrote it off as a 'right strawy epistle', the letter of James has struggled to get a fair hearing in Protestant churches. We suspect that it doesn't teach 'justification by faith', and so insist on reading it through Pauline eyes rather than on its own merits. This is a pity because, as even Luther acknowledged, the letter of

James contains 'many a good saying'.

There are three Jameses in the New Testament. Which of them wrote this letter? James, the brother of John, one of the original twelve disciples, was put to death by Herod in around AD 44 (Acts 12:2), which makes it unlikely that he wrote it. James, the son of Alphaeus, also one of the Twelve, is not heard of again after the resurrection and thus is too obscure a figure to have introduced himself merely as 'James'.

This leaves James, the son of Mary and Joseph, the brother of Jesus and Jude, who was martyred in Jerusalem in AD 62. He was the leader of the Jerusalem church from the mid-40s following Peter's escape from Herod's clutches. He was certainly the leading man by the time of the Jerusalem Council, which was called in around 48 or 49 to settle the issue of what to do with the Gentiles who were flocking into the church (Acts 15:12).

At that Council, James showed himself to be a skilful diplomat, a peacemaker and someone keen to preserve both the purity and the evangelistic cutting edge of the church. He probably wrote the letter containing the decision of the Council that was sent to Antioch. There are notable similarities of language between that letter and the one that bears his name in the New Testament (Acts 15:23–29). The most notable is that the opening greeting is the same in both letters, and different from any other in the New Testament, being just 'Greetings' (the Greek is *chairein*, Acts 15:23; James 1:1). It is entirely possible that the letter of James comes from around this time, maybe a few months before the Council met – say 47 or 48.

There is a view that suggests that the letter, at least in the form in which we have it in our Bibles, is much later – as late as the 80s. But this is unlikely, for the following reasons. There is no reference to the fall of Jerusalem (which happened in AD 70) in the letter. There is no evidence of any dispute between Jews and Gentiles in the church, suggesting that it comes from a time *before* the events that led to the Jerusalem Council. The Jewish tone of the letter suggests that it comes from a time when the Christians still viewed themselves as a movement within Judaism. The recipients appear to be recent converts, and the organization of the church appears to be pretty rudimentary, suggesting an early date.

If it does come from the late 40s, it was written at a crucial time. First, it comes from the time after the martyrdom of Stephen and the scattering of Christians that happened in the wake of that (Acts 8:1–3), but before the controversy over the inclusion of Gentiles in the church that led to the Jerusalem Council (Acts 15:1–2). The dispersion of Christians who chattered and gossipped the gospel wherever they went meant that new churches were springing up all over Palestine without apostolic leadership. The letter appears to be a collection of 'essays' geared towards grounding new Christians in their faith. It could well have been a written form of Bible-based material that James used with new converts in Jerusalem.

Secondly, the letter was written at a time of economic hardship, hence the amount of space devoted in James's teaching to the vital subject of wealth and possessions. Famine came to the whole region between 45 and 47. The majority of his audience would have been rural labourers and peasant farmers, though some probably lived in the coastal trading towns and were business people. They were finding it hard to make ends meet. In the political instability fostered by recession and famine, landowners forced down wages and seized the land of these smallholders, who were unable to keep up with their rents.

This led to growing discontent that strengthened support among the poor for radical groups like the Zealots. James led a church that gave a high priority to sharing and ensuring that no-one was in need. He was concerned to see the same spirit of sharing and generosity in all these new churches springing up around the Palestinian countryside (James 5:1–6). He was astute and politically active. Josephus tells us that James was eventually executed in AD 62 at a time when conservative Jews were weeding out any dissidents in Jerusalem who would sour relations with the incoming Roman governor, Albinus. James was known to have sympathies with those calling for change and especially for greater justice for the poor of Jerusalem and Judea.

In his letter James speaks out against rich, oppressive landlords and on behalf of the poor – language that would not have been out of place at a Zealot rally. Some parts of his letter, though, seem consciously to distance James from the Zealots (1:20; 2:8, 13; 3:13–18; 4:1–4) by espousing the way of non-violence taught by his brother, Jesus. In the tensions of the early 60s, however, any suggestion that you were not a wholehearted fan of the Roman occupation put you in the Zealot camp. That, coupled with James's insistence that Jesus, crucified by the Romans thirty years earlier as a potential rebel, was in fact the Messiah of Israel, cost James his life. He was stoned, as Stephen had been, for blasphemy.

In fact, James's death seems to have caused something of a fuss, which throws fascinating light on the relationship between early Christians and their Jewish neighbours in Jerusalem and more widely in Judea. Josephus tells us that some who were 'strict in their observance of the law' were outraged by the stoning of James. The then high priest, Ananus, who was from the family of Annas and Ciaphas, was a Sadducee, a religious conservative from the aristocratic, priestly élite who ran Jerusalem in league with the Romans.

He was pretty unpopular with the Pharisees and other more militant groups among the Jewish population who were hoping that God would act soon to establish his kingdom, with or without their help (see chapters 15 and 16). James, though a committed follower of Jesus, seems still to have been an observant Jew, worshipping at the temple, and keeping the Sabbath and dietary laws. He seems to have had a good relationship with other Pharisaic groups. It is likely that he shared, argued and debated with them about what it meant to be a Jew, just as Jesus had done, in the hope that his neighbours would come to see that Jesus was indeed the Messiah.

This indicates that though the followers of Jesus in

Jerusalem had beliefs that distinguished them from their neighbours (notably that Jesus was the Messiah, a fact attested by his resurrection from the dead), they had not separated themselves completely from their fellow-Jews. The great separation between church and synagogue happened after the fall of Jerusalem, when Pharisaic Judaism hardened into its rabbinical form, and resentment at the Christians' refusal to join the rebellion against Rome led to their finally being branded as heretics some time in the 90s.

It's possible that though they had their doctrinal and political disagreements with James, the Pharisees' bigger beef was with the chief priests, whose loyalty to Rome was polluting the worship of Israel. The stoning of James was an outrageous injustice that gave them the perfect occasion for counter-attack. So vehement was the reaction of many in Jerusalem that King Agrippa, desperate to keep the lid on simmering Jewish discontent, and no doubt having consulted the incoming Roman governor, deposed Ananus. He would not have taken such a drastic step had James not been such a prominent figure in Jerusalem in the early 60s.

Stick close to God

As well as teaching on wealth and possessions, James covers a number of other basic, vital teachings of the kind needed by new Christians. He tells them to expect suffering and how to handle it when it comes; he teaches about the need to be people who pray; he stresses that genuine faith will lead to works of love and charity; and he speaks of a Christian lifestyle that is marked by submission to God, sincerity and simplicity. Much of what he says is reminiscent of the Sermon on the Mount, as recorded by Matthew in his Gospel, which suggests that James had access to the same collection of Jesus' teaching. He was, of course, writing some time before Matthew completed his Gospel.

Some scholars have suggested that James isn't really a Christian letter at all, but a Jewish text that has had a couple of Christian verses added: namely, 1:1 and 2:1, the two places where Jesus gets a mention. Take these two verses out, and the letter wouldn't be out of place in a synagogue, they say.

But this view fails to take account of the fact that most of what James says is based directly on the teaching of Jesus, even if James is not constantly saying, 'As my brother said ...' For instance, the command to pray without doubting (1:5–6) recalls Jesus in Matthew 7:7–8; the warning of the judge standing at the door (5:9) echoes Matthew 24:33; the prohibition of oaths (5:12) is similar to Jesus' teaching in Matthew 5:34–37; his fierce critique of the rich (5:1–2) recalls Jesus in Luke 6:24; and his use of Leviticus 19:18 – 'Love your neighbour as yourself' – recalls the central place Jesus gave to this commandment in his teaching (see Matthew 22:39; Mark 12:31; Luke 10:37).

Then there are the frequent echoes of the Sermon on the Mount as recorded by Matthew. The exhortation to perfection (1:4) recalls Matthew 5:48; the call to be doers of the word, not hearers only (1:22), recalls Matthew 7:24–27; the warning to keep the whole law (2:10) echoes Matthew 5:19; beatitudes are recalled in 2:13; 3:18 and 4:10 (see Matthew 5:7, 9, 5); the idea that friendship with the world is enmity towards God (4:4) echoes Matthew 6:24; the warning against passing judgment on others (4:11–12) comes straight from Matthew 7:1–5; the certainty that moth and rust will consume earthly wealth (5:1–3) recalls Matthew 6:19; and the use of the prophets as examples of righteousness and suffering (5:10) comes straight from Matthew 5:12.

The sheer number of echoes and quotations means that this has to be more than coincidence. James was evidently a Christian teacher who wanted to apply the teaching of Jesus to the real-life situation of newly converted Jewish believers living out in the rural heartlands of Judea and Galilee.

Walk the talk

James hits the road running. There's no small-talk in the letter. After his cursory greeting he introduces the meat of his teaching, bluntly stating his case and calling his readers to a life of serious discipleship.

At first sight the letter reads like a hotchpotch of disconnected jottings, just one thing after another as James thinks of things he wants to urge on his readers. But closer reading indicates that there is a careful structure to his letter. Chapter 1 seems to function as a collection of introductory headings to a series of longer essay-style sections that make up the rest of the letter. They function almost like the headlines at the top of a TV news bulletin that tell the viewers what to expect in the next half-hour.

The theme of enduring trials and temptations is introduced in 1:2–4, 12–15 and developed in 5:7–11. The topic of wealth and poverty is headlined in 1:9–11 and developed in 4:13 – 5:6. The issue of how we should speak to one another is trailed in 1:19–21 and expanded in 3:1–12. The importance of being doers of what we hear and not just listeners or talkers is introduced in 1:22–26 and developed in 2:14–26. The nature of true wisdom is headlined in 1:5–8, 16–18 and fleshed out in 3:13 – 4:10. The topic of prayer is trailed in 1:6–7 and opened up in detail in 5:12–18.

If James could see the amount of scholarly ink that has been spilled in trying to explain when and why he wrote his letter, what sources he used and who his first readers were, he'd probably be amused, then perplexed and finally angry. These words are not offered for debate, for chewing over with Chardonnay and canapés, and constructing a theology about. These words are for living.

It isn't that James was anti-intellectual. He was clever, quick-witted and well-read, knowledgeable about Jewish history and the writings of the Old Testament – especially the wisdom tradition of Proverbs, Ecclesiastes and Jesus ben Sirach (Ecclesiasticus – a work contained in our Apocrypha). But he also seems to have been familiar with the best of Hellenistic thought. He wrote lively and stylish Greek, and it is clear from Josephus that he was highly regarded among the Jerusalem chattering classes of his day.

But he didn't write to share his ideas, provide after-dinner conversation or launch a new school of thought. He wrote to confront Christians with their need to take Jesus at his word and walk the talk.

How disciples should live

Five major themes stand out in a study of James. The first is prayer. At the heart of the Christian faith is a relationship between the believer and his Lord, Jesus. Everything we do should nurture that relationship, but on-going conversation is essential. So he talks about prayer in 1:5–8; 4:2–3 and 5:14–26 – all crucial places in the letter. But he also talks about the tongue – the organ we pray with – and warns that it's no good praying with it if in the next breath we use it to slay our neighbour (3:1–12, especially verse 9).

Secondly, he talks about faith and works. This is where Protestants, following Luther, get their knickers in a twist over James. Some argue that James is flatly contradicting Paul's teaching on justification by faith by saying that we are justified by works. They point out that the words used in James 2:14–15 seem to be echoing and denying Paul's phrase in Galatians 2:16.

But this is not the case. For a start, it relies on James's letter being written much later than seems likely – that is, well after Galatians, some time in the late 50s or early 60s. And then close inspection of the two texts indicates that both authors are arguing different cases. Paul is responding to those who say that Gentiles have to be Jews in order to become Christians (see chapter 4), whereas James is talking about how we live as Christians. Works are what indicate that someone has faith. James isn't interested in whether we can articulate the doctrine of justification by faith – no doubt he could, in at least two languages. He's interested in whether it makes any difference to the way we live our lives. Does my faith result in my sharing my possessions, feeding the hungry, and showing practical love to my neighbour? If so, then it's probably genuine. If not, then you've got problems.

That's all James is saying (see 1:2–4, 21–27; 2:14–26; 3:13–18). And Paul would certainly agree with him (see Galatians 2:10; 5:6; Ephesians 2:10; 1 Timothy 6:18; Titus 3:14). (On 'justification by faith', see *Discovering James*, pages 101–104, or *Discovering Romans*, page 94.)

Thirdly, James has a lot to say about wealth and possessions. He devotes more space to this subject than to any other in the letter. Our attitude to and use of money and things are key determinants of the quality of our faith. This focus in James probably accounts for its unpopularity rather better than his alleged contradiction of Paul. After all, the church in the consumerist West is as wedded to its economic clout as it is to its doctrinal purity. Hence James's scathing words about the rich, and his blunt teaching that we should share what we have or face the consequences (see 2:1–7, 14–26; 4:1–4, 13–17; 5:1–12).

Fourthly, he focuses on suffering. If we are loyal to Jesus and his way of living, we will suffer opposition and hostility. James is not really talking about illness when he talks about suffering (though see 5:14–15). Rather, he is talking about the opposition we encounter in the world and the struggle we often have with ourselves over living God's way rather than ours. This hurts, says James. It costs to share your possessions and wealth; it hurts to see others advancing ahead you up the career ladder because your focus is elsewhere; it is painful to see family members estranged because they are repulsed by your faith in a crucified Messiah who calls us to the way of peace and poverty (see 1:2–4, 12–15; 4:1–10; 5:1–11, 13–19).

Finally, he talks about the Christian lifestyle as being marked by submission to God, sincerity, openness and simplicity. It is possible to live as Jesus wants us to only if our lives are marked by these three things. We need consciously and continuously to *submit ourselves to God*, which will enable us to live humbly with our neighbours (1:19–21). One of the keys to this is wisdom, understood in its Old Testament sense (3:13–18). We need to be *sincere* (1:26–27). So many Christians are all talk. James reckons it's better to be quiet and let our lives speak before we open our mouths. After all, what comes out of our mouths is so often at odds with what we profess to believe (3:1–12). And our lives need to be marked by *simplicity*. In the midst of a 'me first', money-focused, consumerist culture, we need to find our satisfaction in God and all that he provides us with.

A word to the wise

This is not a comfortable letter. Its directness is embarrassing to those of us used to talking endlessly around the subject. The down-to-earth, practical nature of spirituality is almost rude in a culture that sees spirituality as something other-worldly and mystical. But it is a voice that we need to hear. In a world that is lost in its race to succeed and be top dog, a world where the poor majority are fleeced by a rich minority who live in luxury not even dreamed of by first-century Christians, a world where violence is fed by a desire to own and control more of the finite pool of resources, James is a voice we need to hear. And when we've heard it, instead of talking about it, we need to decide: are we going to live this way or not?

Questions

1. Read James 2:14–26. Does what James say here contradict Paul's teaching that we are justified by faith?
2. Does James actually offer us any advice on how we can control our tongues in 3:1–12?
3. How can we turn good intentions about money into practical action? Does James say anything that helps?
4. Does James offer us a way of making political statements and taking political action?

Mature reflections of an impetuous disciple

1 and 2 Peter, Jude

Do you sometimes wonder whether you're getting anywhere in your Christian life? Do you feel it's all promising starts followed by spectacular failure? Spend some time with Peter, impetuous clown to the court of King Jesus, turned wise old bird. What better than to spend the next six days reading this chapter and 1 Peter, Jude and 2 Peter? You can either follow the plan below or read all three letters right through each day on days 2–5.

Day 1 Read this chapter.
Day 2 Read 1 Peter 1 – 2.
Day 3 Read 1 Peter 3 – 5.
Day 4 Read Jude.
Day 5 Read 2 Peter.
Day 6 Re-read this chapter and look at the discussion questions.
Day 7 Meet with the friends you are reading this book with, have a meal or a drink, and talk through the discussion questions and anything else that struck you through your reading.

The first letter of Peter bursts on its readers with joy (1:3–9). Even with its references to trials and suffering, the text bounces with *joie de vivre* in almost every paragraph. It's somehow fitting that this is the case in something written by

Jesus' muddle-headed right-hand man, who knew the pain of getting it so wrong so often, but who also experienced the sheer delight and freedom of knowing that he was forgiven.

Both the letters that bear Peter's name in the New Testament have had their authenticity questioned. But there is no compelling reason to doubt that 1 Peter came from his pen – or at least his mouth, as he dictated its contents to Silas (5:12). Questions remain about 2 Peter (and its close cousin, Jude), to which we'll return.

Shambling through the first century

By any standards, Peter led a fascinating and eventful life. Originally from Bethsaida, he ran a fishing business in Capernaum on Lake Galilee, up in the Greek-speaking north of Israel. The fact that in his daily business, Peter must have had to have been pretty competent at market-place Greek, puts a question mark over those theories that suggest that an uneducated fisherman (cf. Acts 4:13) wouldn't have been able to write 1 Peter. Greek was widely spoken in first-century Galilee; it was the language of trade with the substantial population of Gentile people in the territory, with whom Peter would have done business daily.

Peter clearly took a lively interest in the future of Israel. He joined John the Baptist's reform movement and got caught up in the excitement that maybe something big was about to break over God's languishing people. John pointed him (with the help of Andrew his brother) to Jesus: here was God's chosen leader who was going to redeem Israel. Did Peter think he was joining an army that would rise against the Roman and Sadducean authorities in distant Jerusalem? Did he think he was throwing in his lot with a reform group like the Essenes, who would make noises from the sidelines and step in when the current order collapsed? We can't be sure. What we can be sure of is that he wasn't joining a religious club with only spiritual concerns. First-century people didn't think that way; spiritual revival meant social revolution and *vice versa*.

All through Jesus' ministry he struggled to grasp what

was going on, however (see *Discovering Luke*, pages 89–92, 125, 155, 187, for the details). He was the first to say publicly that Jesus was the Christ, but refused to countenance the possibility that being the Messiah might involve suffering. He saw Jesus transfigured (something referred to in 2 Peter 1:16–18), and from then on he must have begun to reflect on just who this carpenter from Nazareth really was.

At the end of Jesus' ministry, Peter, completely flummoxed by the way things were turning out, panicked and denied even knowing Jesus, let alone being part of a revolutionary movement. And that would have been it, back home to pick up the pieces of a fisherman's life, had it not been for Easter Sunday and Jesus, risen from the tomb, specifically asking for Peter (Mark 16:7). Peter is back as a disciple, and as one of the leaders of the movement that will carry on Jesus' work (John 21:15–19).

Acts opens with Peter explaining to a stunned crowed of onlookers just what has happened on that first Christian Pentecost. He is the one who does the first miracle in Jesus' name (Acts 3), and he's the first to be arrested (with John) for continuing Jesus' work of proclaiming a new world order (Acts 4). It was Peter who was the first to cross the huge cultural divide between Jew and Gentile and to invite a pagan Roman soldier to participate in Jesus' new world order (Acts 10).

Having had a ministry in Jerusalem, Judea, Samaria and the coastal towns for a decade or so, it seems that Peter travelled north and west from the mid-40s onwards. Some time before the Jerusalem Council (around AD 47; Acts 15), there was an agreement that Peter, James and John would focus their ministry on Jewish people, while Paul and his group would focus on Gentiles (see Galatians 2:9).

Peter certainly spent some time in Antioch, where he learned an important lesson in being consistent and true to what he had learned as a follower of Jesus (Galatians 2:11–21). It's clear that this lesson had sunk in by the time of the Jerusalem Council because Peter uses language very similar to Paul's to describe how people become Christians (Acts 15:7–11). Thereafter, we read of his being in Corinth, probably arriving there with his wife around AD 52. (Paul refers to this in 1 Corinthians 1:12; 3:22; 9:5.) On his way there, he will have passed through the towns and cities of Roman Asia Minor (modern-day Turkey) that he refers to at the beginning of his first letter.

From Corinth, it seems likely that he went to Rome. Following the death of Claudius in AD 54, Jews were returning to that city and Peter probably thought there would be plenty of opportunities to evangelize and help to organize the fledgling church there. It was the early years of Nero's rule, but things were fairly calm, and it seems that Peter and others were able to work relatively unmolested, sharing their faith in Jesus and teaching the believers there, especially the Jewish ones.

It was from Rome – referred to in 5:13 as Babylon, the place of exile (very fitting, given what he writes about) – that Peter wrote his first letter. The biggest objection to accepting that Peter wrote this text is that the Greek is sublime, among the best in the New Testament. An Aramaic-speaking Galilean fisherman couldn't possibly have written it, say some scholars. But there are two major reasons why this isn't necessarily the case. The first is that, as we've seen, from an early age Peter had conversed in Greek. And in the ten to fifteen years leading up to the composition of 1 Peter, the apostle travelled through the Greek-speaking towns and cities of the Roman Empire. His grasp of the language must have got better all the time. One of the finest novelists of the twentieth century was Joseph Conrad, writer of some of the most evocative and flawless English prose. Conrad was a Polish sailor whose second language was French, and who learned English only as an adult. If Conrad could do it in English, why couldn't Peter do it in Greek? The second reason is that Silas, a native Greek-speaking Gentile who helped Paul write some of his letters, lent Peter a hand with this one (5:12).

Encouraging the exiles

The recipients of this letter, scattered little groups of

believers, live all over what is now northern Turkey. Peter describes them as 'exiles of the Dispersion' (1:1). And what he writes is based on a number of Old Testament texts, notably Jeremiah 29:7 and Isaiah 40 – 55. This suggests that his audience was Jewish. But references to not living as the Gentiles do (4:3; cf. 1:14, 18) indicate a mixed readership. After all, the last thing Jewish people did was live as Gentiles! The presence of Silas and Mark, last encountered as part of Paul's entourage, also suggests that Peter had been having more contact with the Gentile mission than the agreement referred to in Galatians 2:9 implied. Almost certainly, in the two decades that had elapsed since that agreement was made, the situation in the churches had changed markedly: congregations were mixed and Christians were paying more attention to people's faith than to their ethnic origins.

Clearly, this is something that Peter wants to encourage. He tells his scattered readers that he has written to them 'to encourage you, and to testify that this is the true grace of God. Stand fast in it' (5:12). What in particular is this grace of God that he's urging them to stand fast in? Their identity in Christ. His readers come from all kinds of backgrounds, Gentile and Jewish; but each of them is part of the new Israel, called out of the world by God and made up of all those who have faith in Jesus.

This is why Peter refers to a lot of Old Testament texts that have to do with who Israel is and how it should live in the world. In particular, he cites texts about or from the time of the exile. And it also helps to explain why there appear to be a number of references to baptism, the rite that marked the beginning of the Christian life, the passing of the believer from his old identity to his new one as a part of God's new Israel (see 1:3, 12, 18, 22; 2:2, 10, 25; 3:21; 4:3). Indeed, some scholars have suggested that 1 Peter is really more a baptismal sermon than a letter – but that's stretching it somewhat.

What Peter has written falls fairly neatly into three sections – much like a sermon. After a lengthy introduction that reminds the readers who they are (1:1 – 2:10), Peter tells his readers how they should live (2:11 – 5:11) and then signs off (5:12–14).

The letter opens with a fantastic panoramic sweep of what God has done for us in Christ (1:3–9) in writing full of passion, gratitude and confidence. And this, he says, was all predicted by the prophets long ago (1:10–12). That phrase opens the door to a flood of Old Testament allusions, echoes and quotations as Peter builds his case.

His readers are God's holy people (Leviticus 11:44–45; 19:20; 20:7 quoted in 1:15). Their new birth (1:3) means they are strangers in this world – hence Peter's extensive use of exile imagery throughout this section and the beginning of the next. The picture of redemption in 1:18–21 echoes Isaiah 43, and 1:22–23 leads up to the quotation of Isaiah 40:6–8 (in 1:24–25). These first readers, says Peter, owe their identity not to their ethnic background or upbringing, but to the fact that God has reached down to them and rescued them from exile and is now bringing them home (1:4–5; 8–9).

To flesh out this picture, chapter 2 opens with Old Testament references falling over themselves to make an overwhelming case for what Peter is saying: Isaiah 28:16 is followed by Psalm 118:22 (used by Peter in Acts 4:11 – clearly a favourite), and then 2:9–10 echoes Isaiah 43:20–21; Deuteronomy 7:6; 10:15; Exodus 19:6; Isaiah 61:5–6; Hosea 1:6, 9; 2:1, 23. Why? To show that what was once true only of ethnic Israel now applies to all those, whether Jew or Gentile, who have faith in Jesus. It is notable that all the Old Testament passages cited come from the two most formative periods of Israel's identity: the exodus (the birth of the nation from slavery in Egypt) and the exile (the rebirth of the nation following punishment for sin). This is the Christian's true identity, says Peter. This is the grace in which we should stand firm (5:12).

And that's all just for starters. Without pausing for breath, Peter launches into the implications of all this. How should Christians live in the world, scattered as they in small communities all over the place, often misunderstood and maligned by their Jewish and Gentile neighbours? That's the theme of the heart of the letter (2:11 – 5:11). The bulk of his teaching is for everyone (2:11 – 4:19), the last little bit particularly for leaders (5:1–11). Each of those two sections is introduced by *parakalō* ('I urge/exhort you').

What is notable about his ethic for exiles is how positive Peter wants us to be about our faith. It's worth shouting about being a Christian, even in places where people laugh at us or beat us up for making too much holy noise. His readers were not being persecuted. The state is basically a benign presence in their lives (2:13–17). It's doubtful that Peter could have written these words five years later when Nero was turning Christians into human torches to light his gardens. But they were suffering at the hands of their neighbours: name-calling, abuse, casual discrimination, being beaten up at night for no reason other than their faith. (This is the suffering Peter has in mind in 1:6–7; 3:16–17; 4:4; 4:12–16.) He urges us not just to put up with suffering but to meet it with grace in full assurance of our faith, and to be ready to account for our hope even when our situation appears hopeless (3:15–16). Peter's ethic is based on Jeremiah 29:7 (2:11–12) and Isaiah 53, used as a prism through which to understand how Jesus' life functions as an example for us in our lives and witness.

His word to leaders indicates that church organization was pretty rudimentary, each congregation led by an elder or two. The dominant picture is that of the shepherd, again derived from the exile, when God came to his listless people as a shepherd (Isaiah 40:11). Leaders are to be gentle pastors who walk humbly with their God (Proverbs 3:34). Peter knows only too well from his own experience that leaders can become big-headed blunderers, prone, like Satan, to arrogance. Resist that temptation by sticking close to God, he says.

Words from the growing dark

What about the other letter that bears Peter's name? And why is most of its central section repeated in Jude's letter? Here we enter difficult terrain. But it's a journey worth taking, because these often-neglected texts have something unique to tell us about our life in this world as Christians.

At first sight 1 and 2 Peter are so different that it seems impossible to think they came from the same hand. But it is possible to see some connections. For instance, both letters speak about the judgment of God; both letters make numerous references to Old Testament texts; both use the example of Noah rescued from the flood (1 Peter 3:20–21; 2 Peter 2:5); and both letters quote freely from works that come from the world of apocalyptic thinking (see chapter 16): 1 Peter 3:18–22 is an impenetrably dense section that really makes sense only if we realize that it is based on a story from *1 Enoch*. (See chapter 16. *1 Enoch* was a very popular, widely read book. As an apocalypse – similar to Revelation – it is concerned with the struggle between good and evil and the eventual victory of Israel's God over the powers that opposed him. See R. T. France's essay in I. Howard Marshall, ed., *New Testament Interpretation*, listed on page 215.)

2 Peter is very much preoccupied with God's coming judgment. It bases its argument on the Old Testament, and quotes freely from apocalyptic material, especially *1 Enoch*. Jude too shares much the same outlook and quotes from a work called *The Assumption of Moses* as well as *1 Enoch*. Jude, the brother of Jesus and James, seems to have been part of Peter's circle (1 Corinthians 9:5), so it's not out of the question that the two of them worked on the material that ended up in 2 Peter and Jude, and that arguing the toss over who wrote what is fairly fruitless.

That being so, we need to ask the usual two questions. Who were the letters for? And what were they about? The first of these is slightly easier to answer in the case of 2 Peter than in that of Jude. Neither tells us who it was written to, but 2 Peter refers to his previous letter (3:1) in such a way that it is entirely likely that he is talking about 1 Peter when he does so. That being the case, 2 Peter's first readers are the same groups of Christians scattered around northern Turkey. We have no idea where Jude's letter was sent.

What seems likely, however, is that Jude was written first. Where the material from Jude appears in 2 Peter (mainly chapter 2), it has been refined to bring out more clearly the central point Peter is trying to make. For instance, Jude speaks of the judgment on Sodom and Gomorrah (verse 7), but Peter adds the nuance that Lot was saved (2:7–8), indicating that God's judgment is not indiscriminate. Peter achieves the same effect by introducing Noah (2:5) to indicate that the godly will be saved even when the whole world appears to be going down the tubes.

It seems that Peter has taken and reworked the material in Jude to comfort and encourage his readers in Asia Minor. 2 Peter as a whole feels a bit like a final statement, a last will and testament, if you like. This makes sense if the letter was written from Rome in the mid-60s – say, 63–65. Nero's persecution of Christians was hotting up. Peter knows his time is short. As a prominent leader he won't escape the fate that has befallen so many others. He refers to this in 1:13–14 (recalling John 21:18–19).

No doubt such news would have saddened and alarmed Peter's readers. It may have caused them to ask why this is happening, and even to express bewilderment that God allows such things. Perhaps some might have begun to have doubts about God's fairness. At the same time, these churches were hearing teaching that contradicted Peter's. Some people were saying that there was a path to enlightenment that avoided suffering. They were saying that notions of a God who judges and holds people to account are old-fashioned and untrue.

Such circumstances could account for the character of 2 Peter, and for its power. For this text is a subtly constructed Christian theodicy – a justification of the justice of God. Now why would a bluff Galilean fisherman write something so apparently abstract and philosophical? Precisely because he knows that these are tough times and that people might stumble. He knows that patience could be wearing thin. Out of a deep pastoral concern for his readers, he wants to encourage them not to give up hope. Despite evidence to the contrary, God *is* faithful, and he *is* coming.

Using a mixture of Old Testament prophecies, good, stirring apocalyptic stories and his own first-hand witness to the glory of Jesus, Peter sets about building a confident picture of God's justice which also undermines the false teachers and warns that judgment awaits both them and any who take their words seriously.

To help in this difficult task, Jude works with him. Between them, they create a powerful text, incorporating some material that Jude has already used some months before. His letter to an unknown group of readers is an exhortation to believers to struggle for the true faith (verse 3). He reminds them that Scripture clearly teaches that those who lead God's people astray will be punished, but those who persevere will enjoy all the blessings of knowing God's salvation. It ends with a wonderful and often-used doxology (verses 24–25).

Hold on, keep holding on

Like 1 Peter, 2 Peter again begins with a rousing call to remember what God has done for us in Christ (1:3–11; memory plays an important role in both this letter and Jude). Again he stresses that what we believe is no novel theory hatched by the chattering classes in some Roman coffee house, but something God has been working on for generations and unveiling to his people through his prophets. We need always to be reminding ourselves of what we have in the prophets and the apostolic testimony, says Peter, because it is Holy-Spirit-inspired truth (1:12–21; cf. 1 Peter 1:10–12).

But there are always those who deny this truth. There were false prophets before, there are false teachers now (2:1), but the basic facts don't change. God can be trusted to give life to those with faith and to judge those who oppose him; God's judgment is both certain and discriminate (2:2–22).

In chapter 3 Peter homes in on what appears to be a particular focus of the false teachers. They say that Jesus isn't coming back. Peter reminds his readers that both the Old Testament and Jesus himself spoke of the 'the day of the Lord'; indeed, 2 Peter 2:5–9 and 3:10 closely echo Jesus' teaching in Luke 17:20–37. If there is any delay in its coming, it is only so that people have a chance to repent and escape the coming judgment (3:9, 15).

Just before he signs off, Peter makes an intriguing statement about Paul's letters (3:13–16). These verses have persuaded some scholars that 2 Peter can't be by the apostle, because it must come from long after Peter's death, from a time when the New Testament canon was being fixed. But this is fanciful. It's not clear how many of Paul's letters Peter knew, but he'd had contact with a number of the churches that Paul had written to. The passage from Paul that best fits Peter's argument here is Romans 2:3–6, verses from a letter Peter would almost certainly have seen, since he was in Rome when it arrived. But what is most noteworthy about this statement is that having spoken of the authority of the Old Testament writings and the apostolic witness, Peter is saying that when that witness is written down, it functions as Scripture just as the Old Testament does. So we need to take it very seriously indeed.

Here then are two pieces of writing, written at a tough time in the early church's life, that urge Christians to remain faithful to their calling because God is faithful. Whatever temporary setbacks and disasters befall us, God can be trusted to act justly. If he has promised to lead through this troubled life to the safe haven of his salvation, that's exactly what he'll do.

Questions

1. What does 1 Peter 2:1–10 tell us about our identity in Christ? What difference does it make to the way we live as individuals and churches?
2. What are the marks of a Christian lifestyle that arise from Peter's teaching?
3. All three of these letters make many references to memory, remembering and recalling. How important to you is remembering what has gone before in your Christian life and in the history of God's people?

Gentle thunder

John's letters

Hectic week? Everything getting on top of you? You need to chill in the presence of the warmest of spiritual guides. In John we find the most glorious refreshment for burned-out souls. Snuggle down over the next six days and read this chapter and 1, 2 and 3 John. Why not read all three of John's letters each day on days 2–5? Alternatively, follow the plan below.

Day 1 Read this chapter.
Day 2 Read 1 John 1 – 2.
Day 3 Read 1 John 3 – 5.
Day 4 Read 2 John.
Day 5 Read 3 John.
Day 6 Re-read this chapter and look at the discussion questions.
Day 7 Meet with the friends you are reading this book with, have a meal or a drink, and talk through the discussion questions and anything else that struck you through your reading.

Everyone, it seems, loves a mystery. TV detective shows, where the hero or heroine has to solve the mystery of 'whodunit', regularly top the ratings. Crime and mystery novels sell in their tens of thousands. *The Mousetrap*, an Agatha Christie mystery, is London theatre-land's longest-running show, having been performed every night since the early 1950s.

The New Testament has its fair share of mysteries too. There are mysterious sayings in the Gospels (such as Jesus warning us not to give jewellery to pigs, or they might trample on it). There are strange events in Acts like the death of Ananias and Sapphira or the effect of Peter's shadow on the sick. But one of the biggest mysteries in the New Testament is: who wrote all the books that bear the name 'John'?

Did the same person write the Gospel, the three letters and Revelation? Did different people, each called John, write them? Is 'John' a name used by several people from the same church or group, in much the same way as 'Peterborough' in *The Daily Telegraph* or 'Pendennis' in *The Observer* is written by a number of people each week?

And possibly most interesting and mysterious of all: how is the 'John' who wrote these works connected to the John who was a follower of Jesus, the brother of James, the son of Zebedee, whom Jesus nicknamed 'Thunderer'?

Back to school

In chapter 2 we suggested that John's Gospel was written in the latter part of the first century by John Zebedee, who by that time was elderly and living in Ephesus. Nearly everyone agrees that the letters of John were written by the same hand that wrote the Gospel.

But there are other views. One very popular idea is that 'John' was a name used by a group of writers who had learned everything they knew of the Christian faith from John Zebedee. Some people have even suggested that there was a school – the first-century equivalent of a theological college – run by this old fisherman or in his name or memory.

This view accounts for the differences between the writings, especially between the Gospel and the letters on the one hand and Revelation on the other. Indeed, the original Greek of Revelation is so different from that of

John's other works that many people suggest that they can't have come from the same person. But this isn't necessarily so, as we'll see in a moment.

There is something going for this idea of group authorship. In 1 John we frequently read phrases like 'we know' and 'we declare' rather than 'I know' and 'I declare'. This could be because the letter reflects the thinking of a group rather than of an individual.

But there are major drawbacks to the idea of a school of John. One is that there is no evidence for its existence. No author writing in the second century, who refers to John, mentions a school or community. These people speak of John the apostle living in Ephesus and refer to him only in the context of being involved in the church, where, of course, he would have had a close circle of friends and fellow-leaders.

A second drawback is that the writer of 1 John says that he is writing of 'what we have seen with our eyes, what we have looked at and touched with our hands'. This is the language of eyewitnesses, not an expression meaning 'all of us at this school have found this to be the case'.

And thirdly, the idea of a school of John doesn't make sense of the fact that the writer of 2 and 3 John refers to himself as 'the elder' and the writer of 1 John refers to his readers as 'dear children', 'beloved' and 'my little children' (1 John 2:1). This is not the language of a group of theological students! Rather, this is the kind of talk that we'd expect from a venerable older leader, a grandfather, writing fondly to people he loves and cares for and has been working with over many years. It is possible to translate 'elder' as 'old man', as if the author is identifying himself by a title that everyone who knows him uses affectionately: 'the old man'.

The final drawback to the idea that John's writings were produced by a school is that Revelation just doesn't fit. This book (which we'll look at in more detail in the next chapter) is clearly the work of an isolated individual, someone cut off from the rest of the church who cannot be with the readers in person, though he wants to be.

Furthermore, Revelation is written by someone with authority, who can credibly claim that his words are inspired by God – that they are true prophecy, the reading of which will bring blessing. He also identifies himself simply as John. Only one of the original apostles could do this without having to justify himself – as Paul was constantly having to do.

But if Revelation is from the same hand as the letters and the Gospel, how come the style is so different? This is difficult to answer with any certainty. But it is not beyond the bounds of possibility that John had the help of a highly educated secretary in Ephesus who turned John's somewhat ragged prose into the flat but competent, simple and uncluttered Greek of the Gospel and letters, whereas alone on Patmos he had to write as best he could.

On top of that, Revelation, being the report of a vision and being written in a particular kind of language comprehensible to those in the know but incomprehensible to their enemies, is a very different work from the Gospel and the letters, which were intended to teach plainly, if profoundly, about Jesus and the Christian life.

Such a view is not without problems, but it is entirely plausible to suggest that the same hand wrote the Gospel, the letters and Revelation, and that that hand belonged to John Zebedee, who ended his days as the leader of, or a leading figure among, a group of churches centred on Ephesus in the final decades of the first century. That is certainly the view we take in this chapter.

The heart of a pastor

The author of 2 and 3 John had a pastor's heart. He was deeply concerned for the health of the churches in his care. Ahead of a planned visit to two of them, he writes to encourage, reassure and warn. The fact that he was planning a visit at all at his age indicates the depth of his concern for these believing communities.

In 2 John he writes to a church which he describes as 'the elect lady and her children'. He encourages them to know and live by the truth of the gospel. He reassures them that they are going on well with the Lord. And he warns them against falling for false teaching (2 John 1, 4).

In 3 John he writes to Gaius, probably a leader of one of John's churches, about a letter he had sent to the church, which has been blocked by a member called Diotrephes. John's passion for the truth means that he must oppose this man, publicly if necessary, so that he does not have an undue influence over younger, more vulnerable believers. (3 John 9–10).

In an age where everything is relative and people rely more on experience than on facts, John's emphasis on the truth, on holding on firmly to the facts of the faith, handed down from Jesus through the apostles, needs to be heard. But it needs to be heard correctly. John is not arguing for cold, unfeeling doctrine. Rather, he is appealing for Christians to unite in love around the agreed truths of the gospel; he is saying that the Holy Spirit inspires both great experiences and deep knowledge, ecstasy and education, love and truth, and that both are focused in John's master and friend, Jesus of Nazareth.

'Sorry, can you say that again?'

Love and truth come into sharp focus in 1 John. This is not so much a letter as a sermon that takes up various themes from John's Gospel, which some people had misunderstood. It is clear from the text that the readers of 1 John were being hassled by people teaching things which appeared to be very spiritual and based on the Gospel, but which were in fact drawn from pagan ideas.

We know what they were saying only by the way John answers them. It seems that the topics that 1 John addresses – fellowship with God, walking in the light, being children of God, being inspired by the Spirit – were all areas of interest to the false teachers. Apparently these people believed that the material world was hopelessly evil and didn't really matter to God. What counted was the 'spiritual' realm, the world of ideas and experiences. To them 'truth' was any knowledge that unlocked the door to great experiences, ideas that freed the hearers from the physical nine-to-five, routine, workaday world that all of us live in.

To these people the great stress of John's Gospel that 'the Word became flesh and lived among us' couldn't be right. God would not get involved in the material order in that way. God was good, and thus could live only in the world of ideas, experience and knowledge (1 John 4:2).

So to get to know God required not the sacrifice of Christ on the cross to bear the punishment for our sins, but the gaining of special, secret knowledge about him that would unlock the door to a whole new world of spiritual experience and intimate union with him. Such knowledge could be acquired only from particular teachers, namely the people who had once been part of John's church but had left and set up their own groups because what they taught contradicted the gospel John had learned from Jesus and the Holy Spirit. This way of understanding God and salvation grew in the second century into the full-blown alternative religion known as Gnosticism (a name derived from *gnōsis*, the Greek word for 'knowledge').

John, of course, was not going to have any truck with nonsense like this. So 1 John takes up and develops themes from the Gospel which emphasize that Jesus came in the flesh, that it is his blood that cleanses us from sin and that we can become children of God, people who live in the light, only through acknowledging our sin, by allowing Jesus to wash us and to make us whole and by living according to his teaching (1 John 1:7).

This very carefully structured letter falls into two halves. The first part, 1:5 – 2:29, could be headed 'God is light'. God is totally holy, pure and good, and therefore we, his people, should live in the light of that, and seek to be holy, pure and good ourselves through following Jesus. Then, under a heading of 'God is our Father', 3:1 – 5:12 tells us that God loves us and is gracious and generous towards us, and that we should therefore live lives that honour him, our heavenly parent, out of gratitude for all he's done for us.

In each half John makes the same five basic points. He tells his readers to renounce sin (1:8 – 2:2; 3:4–9); to be obedient to the truth (2:3–11; 3:10–24); to reject ideas and lifestyles that owe their origin to the world's way of thinking rather than to the gospel of Jesus Christ (2:12–17; 4:1–6); to love, accept and care for one another (1:5–7; 4:7 – 5:4); and to keep the faith they learned from him, especially when under pressure from the false teachers to reject it (2:18–29; 5:5–13).

This is all wrapped up in an introduction (1:1–4) and a conclusion (5:14–21) that assure us that if we live like this we will have fellowship with the Father and with one another, which means that we will be absolutely secure in a difficult world, enjoying the support of brothers and sisters in the church and the constant presence of God through answered prayer.

The wisdom of age

John knows just how hard life is. He's the kind of person who comes and sits with you after church, listens to your struggles and then prays with a simple wisdom that brings a sense of perspective and peace. John calls us back to basics with a gentle but firm voice that has been fine-tuned by experience. The bumptious, arrogant disciple who asked for the most important place at Christ's side has been tempered into the humble, wise pastor who knows that very few things in life are certain, but that Christians need to hold on to those few certainties, no matter what.

His writings – especially 1 John – distil the wisdom of age with a clarity and winsomeness that bring us to the heart of the matter: Jesus is the truth, love is the way, and life is about growing up in the light of those two certainties.

Questions

1. A recently published book on John and his church was called *Thunder and Love*, because this title expresses the two key themes in John's writings: passion for the truth

and compassion for people. Read 1 John and list all the verses that show John's passion for truth and his compassionate feelings towards people. Could these two words, thunder and love, be used to sum up your faith or your church?

2. Read 1 John 1:5 – 2:6. What does this passage teach us about how we maintain our relationship with God and one another?

3. Read 2 John 6. How does the link between love and keeping the commandments work itself out in your life at home and work? In your small group? In your church? (There's lots about this in 1 John to fuel your thinking and discussion.)

Seeing with your ears

Revelation

After the chill, the roller-coaster! The drama of history, the struggles of good with evil, the triumph of the conquering Lamb – like a great movie, John's apocalypse is a feast for the senses as well as the soul. Over the six days we'll read this chapter and Revelation. You can either follow the plan below or read the whole of Revelation each day on days 2–5.

Day 1   Read this chapter.
Day 2   Read Revelation 1 – 5.
Day 3   Read Revelation 6 – 11.
Day 4   Read Revelation 12 – 17.
Day 5   Read Revelation 18 – 22.
Day 6   Re-read this chapter and look at the discussion questions.
Day 7   Meet with the friends you are reading this book with, have a meal or a drink, and talk through the discussion questions and anything else that struck you through your reading.

As we left the cinema, the strains of the rock group *The Doors* and gunfire dying in our ears, I turned to my friend and said, 'Well, what on earth was that all about?' We had been sitting through *Apocalypse Now*, Francis Ford Coppola's epic interpretation of the Vietnam War, and my head was spinning.

As we sat in the pub afterwards, my friend and I tried to fathom out what the film was about. I knew that it was loosely based on Joseph Conrad's *Heart of Darkness*, as well as being about the war in South East Asia that had visited my living-room every evening when I was a teenager.

Coppola's picture made an immediate impact: noise, confusion, fear, anger, laughter and madness. But I found its impact growing, maturing into something deeper and more satisfying as I thought about particular scenes and incidents in the film and tried to grasp how they related to the whole. It also helped to see it again.

John's apocalypse – more commonly called Revelation – is a little like Coppola's *Apocalypse Now*. It is full of weird goings-on: angels with bowls and trumpets, mothers snatched up into heaven, beasts rising from the sea, people identified by numbers, and saints crammed under altars wailing for revenge. It seems to rush from one thing to the next without pausing to allow us to catch our breath. And a common reaction on reaching the end is to gasp for air and say, 'Well, what on earth was that all about?'

Of course, bewilderment has not stopped people from pontificating on what Revelation is about. From Hal Lindsey's *The Late Great Planet Earth* to D. H. Lawrence's *Apocalypse*, all sorts of people have put pen to paper to tell us what the book means.

But what are you?

In one scene in Disney's *Alice in Wonderland* a marvellous mauve caterpillar keeps asking Alice, 'Who are you?' The trouble is that after spending so long in Wonderland, Alice isn't too sure. Many people who read Revelation aren't too sure exactly what it is they are reading. Some read it thinking it is a wonderful, if puzzling, picture of heaven, the victory of Jesus and the future of his people. Others think it's a lucky dip of predictions which can be used like a railway timetable. Some don't bother to read it at all.

Everyone knows that Romans is a letter, Mark is a Gospel and the Psalms are poems. But what is Revelation? It starts like a letter (1:4), claims to be a prophecy (1:3) and is in fact an example of the genre of Jewish and Christian writings known as *apocalyptic*, a type of literature characterized by garish images and concern for God's honour and for the future of his people. (The Greek word in 1:1 translated 'revelation' is the origin of our word 'apocalyptic'; see chapter 16.)

The easy answer to this question, favoured by an increasing number of people, is to say that Revelation is all three: a letter, a prophecy and an apocalypse. But this doesn't help us very much.

Perhaps we should come at it from the other end and ask: 'Who was it written for?' John tells us that he was writing for the seven churches in the Roman province of Asia (the south-western part of what we call Turkey), one of which was in Ephesus (1:4). In the previous chapter we saw that John's ministry was centred on Ephesus. John tells us further that he is writing from Patmos, an island off the coast of Turkey, where, it seems, he had been exiled or imprisoned because of his preaching (Revelation 1:9).

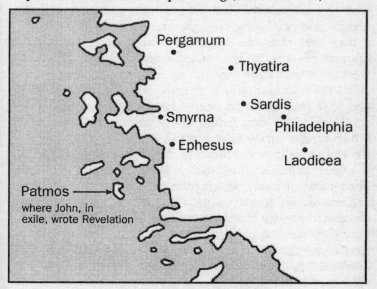

The seven churches of Revelation 2 – 3

On top of that, John describes what he writes as 'the word of God' to these churches. He tells his readers that they will be blessed if they hear and obey the words they read. And he tells them that what he has written will give them insight into what is going on now, both on earth in their own neighbourhoods and in heaven.

Revelation, then, is a letter that brings the word of God to a particular group of people (which makes it a prophecy). But why all the strange and unsettling language? Why the pictures of angels and beasts? Why the constant change of scene between earth and heaven?

Cracking the code

During wartime, military communications are sent in code, so that even if the enemy eavesdrops, they won't be able to fathom out what's going on. Governments invest millions in the technology needed to crack the codes used by other governments.

John's Revelation is written in a kind of code. The form of writing used, which is known as apocalyptic, uses pictures, images and symbols to describe events on the earth in such a way that those in the know will understand but the uninitiated will be left feeling baffled. There are many works written in this way, dating from around 200 BC to AD 200. John's Revelation was probably written between AD 80 and 95 (though some argue that because there is no obvious reference to the destruction of the temple in Jerusalem – which would surely have been of interest to the author of Revelation – the work should be dated prior to AD 70).

One example of the code at work in Revelation is the description of a city which John calls Babylon (Revelation 18). In Jewish thinking, Babylon, which had long since ceased to be a city of any power or importance, had become a symbol for the political oppression and persecution of God's people. This is because it was Babylon that had defeated Israel, overthrown Jerusalem and carted the Jews off into exile in 587 BC.

Now Rome was the dominant power on the world's

stage, and it persecuted the people of God. It had taken Babylon's place, and in apocalyptic writing it was given Babylon's name too. So when John wrote about Babylon in chapters 17 and 18, his readers would have understood that he was speaking about Rome. But when his Roman jailers looked at what he was writing, they would have assumed that he was engaging in a bit of fantasy from Israel's past.

Our trouble with Revelation is often that we don't know the code. Many of its symbols are obscure and difficult, so to get the most from John's work, we need to have a commentary close at hand.

A postcard from the margin

John lived in dangerous times. His congregations faced threats from within through the activities of false teachers, and from without through opposition from Jewish groups and the Roman authorities. He could not be with them to encourage them and to help them keep their eyes on things above and not be crushed by the pressures around them. So he dropped them a postcard from Patmos. He didn't write a letter like Philippians or even like 1 John. Rather, he sent something visual. It seems that he wanted his people to 'see' with their ears and so grasp what was happening around them.

When we read Revelation, it is important for us to remember that this letter was written in response to the circumstances of its original readers and in such a way that it addressed their needs – just as 1 Corinthians responded to particular problems in the church at Corinth. But instead of writing a straightforward letter, John wrote an apocalypse. As we have seen, this was partly to protect the content of his message. After all, one of his key themes is that Jesus is king, and that any others who claim that title (the Roman emperor included) are impostors. Worse, as far as the Romans were concerned, John likened their regime to a beast, a prostitute and the great oppressor Babylon. And finally, he assured his readers that God was coming to sweep this corrupt empire away. In short, John was writing treason, so it's little wonder that he used code.

But the other reason for writing an apocalypse was that John knew that sometimes mere exhortation, however inspired, just isn't enough. People need a picture, a fresh way of seeing the world as it really is, that will inspire them to endure hardship. In this way Revelation is a bit like the section of Isaiah that begins in chapter 40 and ends in chapter 55 and was written to be relevant to the people of God in exile in Babylon. That passage is not a sermon, or a carefully reasoned theology of God's sovereignty, but a poem. There were the people, languishing in exile, abandoning their faith, despairing of ever seeing home again – and God sent a poet.

The reason was simple. What the people needed was to have their eyes lifted to see the world in a different way – to disregard the distorted message that came through the world around them and from their neighbours and even from their own sinful imaginations, and to see the world as God saw it. Isaiah 40 – 55 did that for the people of Israel in exile. And Revelation did it for the seven churches in Turkey at the tail-end of the first century.

Making it make sense

One of my favourite films is *Excalibur*, John Boorman's interpretation of the legend of King Arthur. Every time I watch it I find something new in it. There is a great scene after the grail has been brought to Arthur by Percival, and the restored king rides out to meet Mordred for the final battle. They leave the castle and enter a barren, wintry landscape. But as the king and his knights gallop through a glade, spring breaks out, leaves and flowers appear, and by the end of the scene you can hardly see the horsemen for the blossom. The symbolism is obvious: that the king and the land are one, and the land can flourish only if the king does. But it took me a number of viewings to see it and to recognize the part it plays in telling the story of the film.

Revelation is similar. It needs to be read and re-read in order to make sense. As you re-read it you notice recurring themes, groups of words, numbers and objects. You begin to see how the end relates to the beginning, and how what happens in heaven relates to things happening on earth. Revelation is not a book that yields its treasure on first acquaintance.

It is also important that we learn to handle the symbolism properly. Because John is trying to make his readers see with their ears, nearly everything he says he says by using a picture or a symbol.

First, we need to look for parallels between John's symbols and the pictures we find in the Old Testament. No other New Testament writer alludes to the Old Testament as much as John (though there are no direct quotations). Indeed, he seems consciously to have modelled what he says on the Old Testament, so that everything he writes is a fulfilment of and a climax to what appears in the Hebrew Bible.

Thus the living creatures of chapter 4 are drawn from Ezekiel's vision (Ezekiel 1:10), the white hair of Christ in chapter 1 reminds us of Daniel's picture of the Ancient of Days (Daniel 7:13–14), and the twelve thousand from each of the twelve tribes in chapters 7 and 14 speak of the totality of the people of God.

When we come across a symbol, we should ask ourselves whether John draws it from the Old Testament. But we should not assume that it has exactly the same meaning for John that it had for the Old Testament writer, because John reinterprets everything in his Bible in the light of Christ's coming and coronation.

Secondly, we need to be careful with the details of the symbols. John is an artist who paints in broad brushstrokes. For example, he does not expect us to find a meaning for each of the eyes belonging to the living creatures in chapter 4.

Thirdly, we need to understand the symbols not solely in their own right but also in terms of their context within the whole work. So the beast is not one person and Babylon something else; both are symbols of Rome. John is using a variety of pictures to help his readers to see clearly what they are up against, and he shows them the Roman Empire in all its economic, spiritual and military ugliness (Revelation 17, 18).

Fourthly, we need to guard against thinking that the symbols or pictures can be reduced to simple 'this = that' statements. What John does in chapter 1 is to make a stab at describing what he saw. That's why he keeps saying that things were like other things. If we reduce his pictures to a set of propositions, we end up with John saying that Jesus is an ancient, white-haired man with fluorescent tubes for eyes and a shaft of steel protruding from between his lips.

The final key to making sense of Revelation is to recognize what the book is about. Its chief subject is not the future, the millennium or the judgment. Still less has it anything to do with the forming of the European Union, the Cold War, Saddam Hussein or the barcoding of groceries. Revelation is about Jesus Christ. This is clear from the first sentence. But to reinforce it, John's first vision is of the risen and exalted Christ who is the beginning and the end of the matter, the one who holds the keys to life and death and the one who rules on earth. And his vision of heaven has at its heart the worship of the slain Lamb, the one who has ransomed people from sin by shedding his blood (Revelation 1:5–6; 5:1–14).

Bringing order out of chaos

On the first reading, Revelation just seems to be a mass of happenings and random events. That, of course, is very much like life. The world of Revelation's first readers must have seemed harsh and bewildering. They lived in a world that was decidedly unfriendly towards their new faith. They experienced opposition and persecution that at times must have made them wonder whether there was a God at all, let alone one who was on their side and in control.

But as we read and re-read this powerful work, an order appears – not just on the page but also in our lives. In the midst of the haphazard events, the twists of fate, the good and bad luck, the evil of people and the suffering of the innocent, stands Jesus. He is both the slain Lamb – the picture of innocent suffering and sacrificial death – and the rider on the white horse who conquers and wears the crown (Revelation 5:6; 6:2).

And standing with Jesus are his people. They are not passively observing what's happening; they are in the thick of the battle, and their task is to tell the world who Jesus is so that it may avoid the miseries and terrors of judgment. Indeed, one of the purposes John seems to have in mind in writing Revelation is to tell his people to keep the faith and to keep proclaiming the good news of Jesus, even at the cost of losing their lives, because that will bring glory and great honour to the Lamb who was slain.

Who's calling the shots here?

When Ronald Reagan was shot and wounded early in his first term as President of the USA, confusion reigned. Vice President George Bush told the world, 'I'm in charge.' At the same time Secretary of State Al Haig held a press conference to announce that he was in charge. The upshot was that no-one knew whose finger was on the button of the world's largest nuclear stockpile. For a few hours everyone held their breath: the world was out of control.

The message of Revelation is, 'I'm in charge.' At the end of the first century, as Roman emperors demanded more and more to be worshipped as gods, and as their officials grew more hostile to the Christian church because believers refused to say 'Caesar is Lord', Jesus came to his friend John to remind him who really calls the shots in the universe.

Revelation contains God's final word about human life, history and destiny. That's why it ended up as the last book of the Bible. For just as Genesis opens the Bible with an account of creation, so Revelation closes it with an account of the new creation. Just as the New Testament opens with four accounts of the earthly life and ministry of Jesus, so it closes with an account of Jesus as the king of the universe and the Lord of history.

All that the Old Testament set the scene for is fulfilled in Jesus, says John. All that happens to the church, good and bad, is in the hands of Jesus. Through the church, he proclaims the message, 'I'm in charge. Look to me and live.' To him the church in worship and adoration says, 'Amen. Come, Lord Jesus.'

Questions

1. John refers to Jesus as 'the Lamb of God' twenty-eight times in Revelation (5:6, 8, 12, 13; 6:11, 16; 7:9, 10, 14, 17; 8:1; 12:11; 13:8, 11; 14:1, 4, 10; 15:3; 17:14; 19:7, 9; 21:9, 14, 22, 23; 22:1, 3). What do these verses (and the surrounding text) tell us about who Jesus is and how he fits into God's plans for his world?

2. A key theme of Revelation is that of *witness* (1:5; 2:13; 3:14; 11:3; 15:5; 17:6; the Greek word for 'witness' is where our English word 'martyr' comes from) and *testimony* (1:2, 9; 6:9; 11:7; 12:11, 17; 19:10; 20:4; 22:16). what do these verses tell about the ministry of the church and individual Christians in a hostile world?

3. In 6:17, in the midst of a picture of the chaos and violence of the world we live in, the people cry, 'Who can stand?' Reading 7:1–17, tease out how it is that John could say that Christians *can* stand (7:9). These verses tell us about God's role and our role in ensuring we can stand in the midst of turmoil, opposition, trials and difficulties.

4. 'I can't believe in a God of love because of the suffering in the world.' Is there anything in Revelation that might help us to answer this common objection to belief in God's care and concern for his world? Clues might be found in the letters to individual churches (1 – 3), the worship of heaven (4 – 5), the vision of the two beasts and the Lamb (13 – 14), and the closing vision of Satan's downfall and the new heaven and new earth (20 – 21).

PART TWO

The essential New Testament user's guide

Jesus' world

Most British people don't know much history. Perhaps we're aware of Churchill and the Second World War. But we know little about the Corn Laws, Chartism, John Wilkes, the Levellers, the Act of Supremacy or the signing of Magna Carta. And yet these events have shaped us and made us the people we are.

Jesus grew up in a community very conscious of its history, of the events that had moulded it and of the people who made it what it was. Shakespeare likened history to a tale told by an idiot, full of sound and fury, signifying nothing. Maybe we share his view. To Jesus and his community, history was a tale told by God, full of sin and salvation and working its way to a climax: the coming of God's kingdom.

Striking a blow for freedom

From about 530 BC onwards the people of Israel drifted back from exile. Nehemiah rebuilt Jerusalem from the 440s. Many Jews never bothered to return. Instead, they stayed in the East or made their way west to Turkey, Greece and Italy, living in what came to be known as the Diaspora.

For those who did return, life wasn't great, except for one glorious period that people in Jesus' day looked back to as a golden age and an inspiration to all freedom-loving Jews.

The Persian Empire of Cyrus and Artaxerxes, which allowed the Jews to return to their land, fell to the expanding Greek Empire of Alexander the Great, with Palestine coming under his authority in 332 BC. When Alexander died at the tender age of thirty-two, his empire was torn in two by rival generals. The Ptolemies, based in Egypt, held sway in the south, while the Selucids, based in Syria, held sway in the north. Palestine was the meat in the sandwich between the two power blocs.

To begin with, it was ruled by the Ptolemies, who were live-and-let-live kings. They allowed the Jews, especially around Jerusalem, a great deal of autonomy, provided they paid their taxes. But in 200 BC Palestine was won from the Ptolemies by the Selucids, who were more aggressive rulers. Life for the Jews got harder.

Life became intolerable under the Selucid ruler, Antiochus IV Epiphanes, whose policy was to force all his subjects to adopt Greek ways. The Jerusalem aristocracy went along with this, but the priestly families and the rural peasant farmers resisted. In 167 BC Antiochus set up a statue to the pagan god Zeus in the temple in Jerusalem and banned the practice of the Jewish religion in Judea.

This sparked off a full-scale revolt, led by Judas Maccabeus, 'the Hammer'. So successful was this uprising that the pagans were driven out of the land and Judea

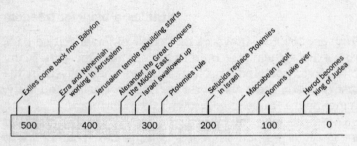

The history of Israel

became self-governing. The temple was cleansed and restored in 164, an event still celebrated by Jews today in a festival called Hanukkah.

All roads lead to Rome

At this time the Roman Empire was gaining in strength, and it made sense for the tiny state of Judea to have a powerful friend. So in 139 BC it signed a treaty with Rome which guaranteed its protection and enabled it to expand. Over the next fifty years the state grew to the size it had been under King David, capturing first Samaria, then the southern Idumean kingdom and then the northern territories of Galilee and the Decapolis, as well as the coastal towns. Its policy was to reverse what the Selucids had done, removing Greek cultural and religious influences and almost forcing people to practise the Jewish religion – which most of them were only too happy to do. Galilee, however, remained full of pagan influence and culture, so much so that it was known in Jesus' time as Galilee of the Gentiles.

But there were political problems: squabbles and fights between rival groups threatened to reduce the country to anarchy and civil war, and in 63 BC the Romans stepped in and took control of the whole region.

Rome liked, wherever possible, to rule through local

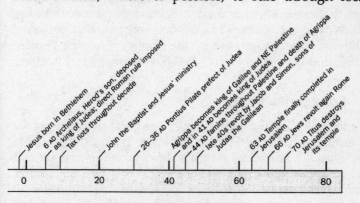

The history of Israel

kings. So, when it found a powerful and loyal royal family in Idumea, it made them kings of the country. The most famous member of this dynasty is Herod the Great, king when Jesus was born (Luke 1:5).

Herod sought to win the popularity of his new subjects by rebuilding their temple in Jerusalem and making it one of the wonders of the world. It was still being finished off during Jesus' ministry. Herod did a lot of other public works, but he was an unstable and paranoid man, convinced that every dark corner contained a group plotting his overthrow. He put to death many of his rivals, including many of his own children. So it is no surprise that, on hearing of Jesus' birth, he had all boys under the age of two in Bethlehem killed for fear of losing his throne to the new rival (Matthew 2:16–18).

When Herod died, his kingdom was divided among his sons, Herod Antipas, Philip and Archelaus. While the first two were tolerated, Archelaus was totally unacceptable to the people of Judea. A delegation of Samaritan and Jerusalem aristocrats (an unlikely and somewhat unholy alliance, given the animosity between the Jews and the Samaritans) went to Rome to appeal to the Emperor Augustus to remove Archelaus. (These events lie behind Jesus' parable of the pounds in Luke 19:11–27.)

To keep the peace, Augustus deposed Archelaus, exiled him to France and imposed a Roman governor of Judea, which was not really what anyone wanted. During Jesus' ministry, Judea was ruled by the Roman governor Pontius Pilate, and Galilee by Herod the Great's son, Herod Antipas.

A bit of a curate's egg

Roman rule, like the curate's egg, was good in parts. On the plus side, within the Empire there was peace, the so-called *Pax Romana*. The crime rate was low, with the seas by and large cleared of pirates and the highways free of bandits. The courts operated efficiently and justice was administered in a relatively even-handed way. The roads were good and trade flourished. Many people prospered in the single market that stretched from France all the way to Turkey and North Africa.

The down side was that the Jews were no longer in control of their destiny, and they had to pay taxes twice. Every Jewish man had to pay a tax for the upkeep of the temple, and tithes to keep the priests and Levites in food and clothes. On top of that, the Romans imposed taxes at three levels: a poll tax, paid by everyone in the Empire except Italians and Roman citizens (so Paul would not have paid it, but Jesus would); a land tax levied on all owners of land and when land changed hands; and indirect taxes such as customs duties and sales taxes.

It is reckoned that the average Jewish man saw about 40% of his income go in taxes. So, not surprisingly, taxation caused huge amounts of aggro, debates about whether it should be paid or not, and occasional armed uprisings.

Possibly the biggest bone of contention was the method the Romans used to collect their taxes. Instead of their own civil servants, they contracted the job out to freelance tax-collectors who made a lump-sum payment to Rome for the tax due on their patch and then collected that amount back plus a bit extra from the hapless citizens. Tax-collectors had all the social standing of prostitutes, lepers and serial killers in first-century Palestine, as we see in the story of Zacchaeus (Luke 19:1–10).

There was one other benefit of being part of an empire, though this was an accidental spin-off from Alexander's conquest. It was that nearly everyone spoke the same language. Latin was the official language of the Roman Empire; but in the eastern half of the Empire few non-Romans spoke it, though it was the language of the lawcourts. Greek was the language everyone spoke in the market-place. So whether you lived in Alexandria in Egypt, Ephesus in Turkey or Nazareth in Galilee, you would have known enough Greek to get by.

This means that Jesus would almost certainly have been able to speak three languages. His everyday teaching and conversation with people in Galilee and Judea would have been in Aramaic. Conversations with people in the

Decapolis or with Romans, especially at his trial, would have been in Greek. And when he read in synagogue, he would have spoken Hebrew, the language of the Old Testament (Mark 5:41).

People of the land

Jesus lived in a world where most people earned their living from the land or the water (around the shores of the Sea of Galilee). If they weren't farmers, they were fishermen or craftsmen who supplied agricultural implements or household goods.

It was a world without TV or newspapers or rapid communications; a world where news spread by word of mouth, where people told stories and kept in touch with events through travelling business people and market traders who passed through their village.

There was not a lot of leisure time. The Jewish Sabbath (Saturday) was a compulsory day off for the Jews. The whole family would gather at the synagogue to worship God, hear the reading of the Law and the Prophets and maybe talk about what it all meant. Of course, there was also probably a lot of talk about crops, herds (generally very small), the weather, taxes and tax-collectors and the family. Perhaps there would be talk of a forthcoming wedding, or the fact that a son or daughter was now of marriageable age and a suitable partner was being sought.

The rest of the week was hard graft. From dawn till dusk every member of the family would muck in with chores around the house and farm. If the business of the household was manufacturing (such as carpentry), even the youngest would have a role tidying up or making sure that the few animals the family owned were fed and watered.

So it's not surprising that special occasions were an excuse for a party. Weddings lasted a week, with feasting and exchanging gifts (John 2:1–11). Banquets, which were rare, and were hosted and attended only by the wealthiest in the community, were spectator sports. The guests would recline at low tables in the open courtyard of the house, being waited on by servants who brought not only the food but also warm, scented water for the diners to wash their hands in every so often. A large animal – at least a sheep but at big feasts a cow or ox – would be roasted over an open fire as the guests gathered. Those not invited crowded round the gate to the house, drooling over the sumptuous food and playing 'spot the celebrity'. Perhaps the guests would include the synagogue ruler, or a prominent scribe, or the local Roman centurion (Luke 7:37–50).

Other excuses for a celebration would include finding something precious that had been lost, like a sheep or a coin, or paying off the debt incurred to a money-lender because of a poor harvest or broken plough.

It was a world of colourful characters: tax-collectors, merchants from exotic lands, kings, robbers, victims, helpful travellers, prostitutes, sinners, debtors and insufferably snooty religious people. It was a rich source of material to the gifted preacher looking for illustrations for his teaching about the kingdom of God. So it's not surprising that this world crops up in vivid colour in all its humour and sorrow in Jesus' parables.

14

The Jewish religious calendar

At the heart of Jesus' world as he grew up, worked as a carpenter and travelled as a preacher, were the synagogue and temple. The synagogue was the centre of community life. Every substantial village had one. Not only was it a place of worship on the Sabbath (Saturday), it was also the place where Jewish boys learned to read and recite the law prior to their *bar mitzvah* – the ceremony on their thirteenth birthday in which they became a son of the law, an adult member of their community (Luke 4:16).

Jesus was faithful in his attendance at synagogue and in his participation. Synagogue was run not by priests but by laymen. No sacrifices were offered; the services consisted rather of the reading of the Law and the Prophets, a sermon, prayers and worship based around the singing of psalms.

While every town had a synagogue, there was only one temple. It was in Jerusalem, and, as rebuilt by Herod, it was a vast and wonderful building, visible for miles around with its gold dome radiant in the sunlight.

Every day priests served in the temple, offering sacrifices at morning and evening worship. They also made a daily offering for the emperor, but this practice ceased in AD 66 with the outbreak of the revolt. From time to time private sacrifices were made on behalf of individuals (Luke 18:10).

The temple was the focal point of the three big festivals in the Jewish year. The Feast of Passover (including the Feast of Unleavened Bread) happened in March/April and cele-

Major festivals of the Jewish year

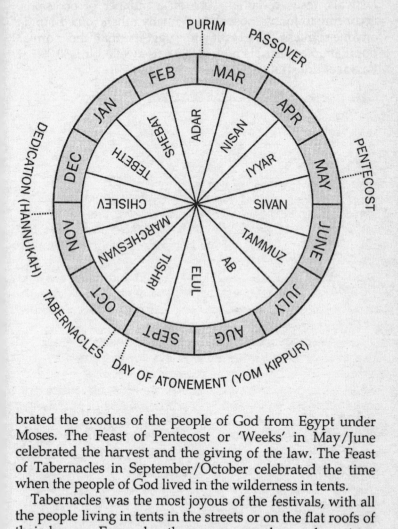

brated the exodus of the people of God from Egypt under Moses. The Feast of Pentecost or 'Weeks' in May/June celebrated the harvest and the giving of the law. The Feast of Tabernacles in September/October celebrated the time when the people of God lived in the wilderness in tents.

Tabernacles was the most joyous of the festivals, with all the people living in tents in the streets or on the flat roofs of their houses. Every day there were parades as the priests brought water into the temple in remembrance of God's provision of water in the desert, and every evening great lights were lit to commemorate God's presence in the pillar of fire.

Every Jew was expected to go to Jerusalem for these festivals. Jesus certainly went on a number of occasions, according to John's Gospel. How many others joined him is anyone's guess. One estimate suggests that the normal population of Jerusalem of 30,000 was swelled to 180,000 at Passover time (John 7:1–10).

15

Sects and parties

First-century Palestine was full of groups, sects, parties and gangs. They were not political parties as we have them today. They were more like debating and pressure groups – collections of people coming together to promote a certain view of life, and especially of what it meant to be a Jew, a member of the covenant people of God in their time and situation. Some of these groups we come across in the Gospels, others we don't.

The main group we meet in the Gospels is the *Pharisees*. They get a really bad press from Christians. We tend to see them as fussy hypocrites, but in fact they were the charismatic evangelicals of Jesus' day.

They date from the period of the Maccabean revolt, and their name probably means 'separated'. They took the law of God very seriously and sought to live by it, applying it to every detail of their daily lives. These applications became a sort of supplementary law handed down from teacher to pupil and debated in small groups or fellowships. Their aim was not to invent rules that couldn't be kept, but to be as practically holy as possible (Luke 6:1–2).

The Pharisees were generally not priests. Most of them were ordinary men who wanted their faith to touch the whole of their lives. They were very influenced by apocalyptic ideas (see chapter 16), especially by the notion that God would break into history and establish his kingdom through his anointed king, the Messiah. They believed in the resurrection, in the Holy Spirit and in angels – all quite new ideas within Judaism. They also believed that membership of the people of God was based on grace – God's choice through the covenant – and not on works. 'Covenant' and 'election' were key words in their theology.

They were also very political. It was impossible to separate theology and politics in first-century Israel. They resented Roman rule, which they felt polluted God's land and meant that the people languished in a continuing exile: although they were back in the land, they were not free from foreign interference. Worse, Yahweh, their covenant God, was not their king; Caesar was. They boiled with indignation against pagan rule and longed for God to act – probably through an anointed Messiah, a king who would lead them in revolt and triumph like David and Judas Maccabeus. When the kingdom came, they thought, the Romans would be driven out and the land purified; the exile would at last be over.

The Pharisees were very popular and people looked up to them. After the fall of Jerusalem in AD 70, they became the dominant group in the rebuilding of Judaism without a temple.

There were two main groups of Pharisees, following a split some time in the reign of Herod over interpretation of the law. Rabbi Hillel took a 'live and let live' approach to the politics of his day. He would not rock the boat that Herod and the Romans were riding, providing the Pharisees were left unmolested to practise their religion. Rabbi Shammai was more hard-line. The Torah (the law of Israel) demanded that the people be free from the yoke of the Gentiles – and that included the half-breed Herod and his clan. The Shammaites appear to have been in the ascendancy throughout the first century until the fall of Jerusalem in AD 70. Paul was almost certainly a Shammaite, burning with zeal for the traditions of his people to the extent of persecuting the church, which he saw as a betrayal of everything Israel was about (see chapter 21).

Alongside the Pharisees were the *scribes* (*teachers of the law* in some versions). As the name suggests, these people were connected with books and learning. They not only wrote, but also studied and taught the law. Their role was to preserve the good traditions of the people of God and to guard them against heresy. Most were probably priests or from priestly families. By Jesus' time there were so many priests that there had to be a rota for temple duties. Most would serve for only a few weeks a year. The rest of the time they spent in study and teaching.

Jesus' beef with these two groups was their snobbery and exclusiveness, their belief that only they had God's ear, only they took discipleship seriously, only they were part of God's in-crowd. Their sin was pride and a judgmental, condescending attitude to anyone not as perfect or privileged as them. He also thought they were wrong politically. They believed the future lay in armed rebellion against Rome. But Jesus taught that God's kingdom would not come through the sword; rather, it would come through his way of love, especially love for enemies. Read the Gospel of Luke with that in mind and see how it colours your understanding of Jesus' encounters with the Pharisees.

Linked to the Pharisees in the Gospels – in a somewhat unholy alliance – were the *Herodians* (Mark 3:6; 12:13; Matthew 22:16). As their name suggests, they were supporters of the Herod family's claim to be rulers of Israel. They were in a delicate position, as their question over paying taxes shows. On the one hand they would have liked their dynasty to be ruling Palestine in its own right. On the other, given the power of Rome, they knew that the Herod clan's only hope for staying in power was to keep in with Caesar.

This makes them unlikely allies with the fiercely nationalistic Pharisees, except that they clearly found the politics of Jesus to be such a threat that they were prepared to forge alliances with anyone to get rid of him. Jesus, in proclaiming the coming of the kingdom of God through his ministry, was claiming that Herod was not the true king. If, as they thought, he was another revolutionary 'messiah', they felt that if he came to power their days would be numbered. So a short-term alliance with the scribes and Pharisees seemed the lesser of two evils.

The final group we come across in the Gospels and Acts is the *Sadducees* (Mark 12:18; Acts 23:6–11). These were the opposite of the Pharisees. They were part of the ruling élite, Judea's aristocracy. Their power base was the temple, where most of them were priests. They were very conservative in their views, rejecting such new doctrines as the resurrection or belief in angels. And they considered only the first five books of the Old Testament (the Torah) to be God's Word; the other books were interesting but not authoritative. They weren't very popular among ordinary Jews. Many saw them as too friendly with the Romans, too keen to feather their own nests. No-one mourned their passing with the destruction of the temple in AD 70.

Taking it to extremes

Two other groups are worthy of mention. They fill out the picture, showing the extremes in the debate about what it meant to be the people of God in first-century Judea.

The first group was the *Essenes*. They were a small, élitist sect who lived all over Israel. Their main base was a fortified monastery by the Dead Sea. We knew virtually nothing about them until 1948, when some documents (now known as the Dead Sea Scrolls) were discovered in caves at a place called Qumran.

What they revealed was a group who believed that God would come soon and establish the kingdom, and that only the very purest of Jews would be worthy to enter it. They thought the temple in Jerusalem and the priests who worked in it were hopelessly corrupt, and they dreamed of the day when they would take it over and offer pure sacrifices to God.

As well as living lives of celibacy, they devoted themselves to reading the Scriptures and producing commentaries on them for their own use. They also trained for war, in anticipation of the day when they, the Sons of Light, would fight alongside God and his angels against the Sons of Darkness, the Romans. In the event, they appear to have been wiped out in AD 70.

The second group are usually known as the *Zealots*. This isn't strictly accurate. The Zealots were one of a number of groups (including some groups of Pharisees) who believed that God needed a helping hand in purifying the land and establishing his kingdom. These groups were the militants in first-century Palestine, the Hezbollah of their day. They were close to all the Pharisees theologically and politically. And they believed that armed struggle was not just an essential component of being a true son of the law, but something they must actively stir up.

Through the first half of the century, such groups sprang up from time to time. Judas the Galilean led a tax revolt in AD 6; Barabbas was involved in an insurrection at the time of Jesus' crucifixion; Theudas tried to start a revolt in the early 40s in the area around the River Jordan. In the 50s there flourished a group called the Sicarii ('the dagger men'), of whom Eleazar and 'the Egyptian' were the most notable. They carried out assassinations and generally got up the Romans' noses.

First-century Israel was a land in ferment. Although life carried on much as normal in most parts of the country, and although it's probably true to say that most people weren't part of any gang, there was an undercurrent of discontent, a desire for something better, a longing that God would come. No wonder Jesus touched a nerve with ordinary people. No wonder the church found willing ears among marginalized and expectant Jews before exploding into the Gentile world.

6

The apocalyptic outlook

The most popular reading-matter in first-century Palestine was a form of fantasy writing known as apocalyptic. These works, a sort of cross between Harry Potter, science fiction and soap opera, spelled out Israel's hope in terms of God's decisive intervention in the world to establish his rule over all the nations and vindicate Israel's loyalty to him.

Life for Israel in the first century wasn't great. People still felt themselves to be in exile. For although they were physically located in the land of their ancestors, they were not free to run their own affairs; they languished under Roman domination. They longed for God to step in and fulfil all the hopes and promises contained in the great Old Testament prophets, especially Isaiah and Ezekiel.

Over a period of about three hundred years (from 200 BC to AD 100), as thinkers and activists mused on these writings, they created a new way of telling their story that kept their hopes alive. This form is called *apocalyptic*.

Catching the drift

Usually written in the voice of some long-dead hero, such as Baruch, Ezra or Enoch, these stories shared certain characteristics.

1. *The future is revealed to the writer by an angel.* This usually takes the form of a vision in which the author asks, 'What's happening?' and 'What's going to happen next?'

The angel's reply takes the form of a revealing (the word *apokalypsis* in Greek means 'unveiling') of God's master plan, referred to as a mystery or secret known only to God and his messenger.

2. *A dualistic view of creation.* There is a rigid separation between earth and heaven and between the current age and the age to come. The gulf between earth, where people live, and heaven, where God rules, is bridged in apocalypses by the angelic messenger, though sometimes the writer is invited to see for himself what is happening in the otherwise hidden and unknowable heavenly realm. Apocalypses look forward to the time when God intervenes to end the current age, with all its misery and pain, and begin the new age of justice and joy without an overlap between the two.

3. *The prevalence of evil.* This age in apocalyptic writing is characterized by the rampant nature of evil. The texts are full of references to Satan, demons and evil forces, to beasts lurking behind oppressive human rulers and to the persecution of all who seek to follow Yahweh, Israel's God.

4. *The universal nature of Israel's hope.* Apocalypses foresee a day when Yahweh will rule over the whole earth. The age to come will be a time of justice, ushered in by the judgment of the nations and the resurrection of all God's faithful servants.

Keeping hope alive

Apocalypses weren't fantasy stories read for entertainment. They were manifestos for action. The book of Daniel, for instance, was used as a clarion call for Israel to stand firm at the time of the Maccabean revolt because God was on their side (see chapter 13).

By the first century, with Israel again under foreign domination, apocalyptic kept the nation's hopes alive. It gave them the hope that God's kingdom would come soon. It told a waiting people that a Messiah – sometimes referred to as 'the Son of Man' after Daniel 7:13 – would lead the nation to freedom and establish the rule of God over the world. And it gave them the hope that even if they died without seeing this kingdom arrive, they would be raised to enjoy life in it after God has intervened and consigned the forces of evil to oblivion. No wonder they prayed every day, 'May the kingdom come in my lifetime.'

Not surprisingly, then, when John the Baptist came saying that 'the kingdom of God is at hand', the nation pricked up its ears. When Jesus took up the call and began to flesh out what the kingdom would be like, he caused a feverish debate and excited the people's expectations.

Jesus was an apocalyptic figure. He declared the kingdom of God, expressing his understanding of it in the language of the two ages (Mark 3:29; 10:30; 11:14). He saw the present age as deeply influenced by demonic forces (Mark 3:22–26; Matthew 4:11), and his ministry as the beginning of their defeat (Luke 10:18). He spoke of the life to come being preceded by the resurrection (Mark 12:25), and of his own resurrection as a vindication of his ministry (Mark 8:31; 9:31). He saw the imminent end of this age and the arrival of the new age as tied up in his activity, especially in his death and resurrection. He saw himself firmly as Daniel's 'Son of Man' (Mark 9:1; 13:24–27; 14:61–62).

But Jesus introduced two crucial revisions into the typical apocalyptic outlook, and these spilled over into early Christian teaching:

1. *An overlap between the two ages*. (This is referred to as 'realized eschatology', meaning that the last event [the *eschaton* – talk of which is called *eschatology*, the doctrine of last things] has begun to happen, but has not been completed.) Apocalyptic thought foresaw that the present age would continue until God stepped in and wrapped it up before starting the new one; there would be no overlap at all between these two periods. Jesus, however, said that the kingdom was both here now *and* still coming (Luke 4:16–21; 7:18–23; 11:20; 16:16; 17:21; 13:22–30; 14:15–24; 22:15–18). The new age was breaking in before the old age had run its course. And this would be seen in the fact that Jesus' resurrection pre-dates the general resurrection and the final judgment.

2. *Caution about timing*. Apocalypses often read like

railway timetables, cataloguing vast numbers of events that must occur in a certain order before the present age is ended and the new one begins. Jesus said it was all a lot less predictable than that. Part of the reason for this is that the life of the new age had already spilled into the old age, muddying the waters somewhat. Another reason is that Jesus was keen to stress that we couldn't take comfort in the fact that, just because a whole list of things hadn't happened yet, the judgment was still way off. We need to be ready all the time, because the day will come like a thief in the night (Luke 12:35–40; 13:1–5; 21:34–36).

Following Jesus' lead

As the New Testament writers struggled to grasp the significance of Jesus' ministry, their apocalyptic outlook helped them considerably. But at the same time that outlook was radically affected by Jesus' teaching, death and resurrection.

The Christian hope remained the same as that of mainstream apocalyptic, namely that Yahweh would soon step in to establish his kingdom over the world, raise his faithful people to a new life and call the nations to account in a final judgment. But now that hope was focused on a historical figure. Instead of vague ideas about a mysterious 'Son of Man', the Christians knew that God would establish his kingdom through Jesus, whom he had made both Lord and Messiah as a result of his resurrection (Acts 2:36; 17:29–31).

They knew other things as well. In five major areas Christian teaching was moulded by an apocalyptic outlook that was radically amended in the light of Jesus' ministry.

1. *Justification*. In apocalyptic thinking, justification for the righteous (by which they meant faithful Jews) would take place at the last judgment at the close of the present age. But because the kingdom of God had begun to break into the world through Christ and especially his cross, Christians proclaimed that justification is available now to any and all who put their trust in God's Messiah, Jesus. Justification

was closely bound up with membership of the people of God. Apocalyptic thought reckoned that only Jews could be vindicated on the day of judgment. Christians realized that the cross opened membership of God's people up to Gentiles as well. Hence those who are justified through faith in Jesus are members of the people of God drawn from every nation (see Romans 1 – 5).

2. *The coming of the Holy Spirit.* The Spirit is an eschatological gift (Joel 2:28–29; Ezekiel 36:26–28). Apocalyptic writers spoke of it in relation to life in the new age. But the Spirit had been poured out before the end of the present age (Acts 2:1–37), as a taste of the life to come. This is why Paul refers to the Spirit as the firstfruits (Romans 8:23) and the down-payment (Ephesians 1:14) of the life we will enjoy in the age to come.

3. *The certainty of resurrection.* Belief in the resurrection, which surfaced in Daniel, was a product of the apocalyptic outlook. Naturally, the New Testament writers shared it. But their faith in it was sharpened by the resurrection of Jesus, to which many of them were witnesses. Hence Paul is able to speak of Jesus as the forerunner of all who believe in him (1 Corinthians 15).

4. *The defeat of the principalities and powers.* The apocalyptic outlook had brought belief in the powers of darkness into sharper focus than before. In Jesus' ministry these powers were all too evident in the opposition he faced. The New Testament writers soon came to see Jesus' cross as the decisive battle-ground where these hostile forces were disarmed and stripped of their power (see especially Colossians). This meant that when John composed his apocalypse, he was able to show both the reality of the demonic powers that lie behind false religion and abusive political power, and the certainty of Jesus' victory over all these forces and their ultimate destiny in a lake of fire. It also meant that Christians were able to declare a gospel of freedom not only to Jews but also to Gentiles, because in Jesus all bondage to hostile forces is broken.

5. *Timetables.* Most apocalyptic authors assumed that theirs would be the last word before the world as they knew

it ended. A few (notably *2 Baruch* and *4 Ezra*) entered a note of caution, suggesting that although it was imminent, the end of the current age might be delayed – though the reasons for such delay were vague, at best. We have already noted that Jesus cautioned against apocalyptic timetables, stressing the need for people to be ready all the time for the end of this age and the arrival of the age to come. But the New Testament also hints at a delay before God wraps things up, most notably in 2 Peter 3 and Revelation 6 – 11. The reason for this delay is spelled out clearly: that the church may proclaim the good news of Jesus to the world (see Luke 21:13; Mark 13:9–11).

We live in the overlap between the two ages. This results in a tension between the 'now' and the 'not yet' of the life we enjoy in Christ. Now we are justified and filled with the Holy Spirit. But we are not yet freed from the pain of living in a world of sin and opposition. Now we know the fellowship of living as part of a new community of people drawn from all around the world. But we are not yet freed from the tensions and conflicts that arise when people from differing cultures try to live and work together. Now we know a measure of healing, but we are not yet made whole and mature after the likeness of the human stature of Christ (see Philippians 3:1–17).

And this overlap is a world of opportunity. As Paul spelled out at the beginning of Romans, we declare the good news of a coming king, Jesus, son of David, Son of God, raised from death to establish his kingdom (Romans 1:1–5). One day every knee shall bow to him (Philippians 2:11). Now, through the preaching of the gospel, every person is invited to bow the knee to him voluntarily and experience a foretaste of the life to come.

A brief history of the rise of Christianity

Jesus was born at the tail-end of the reign of Herod, when Augustus was emperor, probably around 4 BC. His birth was no big deal as far as the Romans were concerned, though Herod was sent into a blind panic by it. Jesus grew up in a world where Roman power was taken for granted, but in a country where people longed to be free to govern themselves (Luke 2:1–2; Matthew 2:1–11).

John the Baptist, a cousin of Jesus, began his ministry around AD 28. He was like something out of the Old Testament: hairy, wild, fiery, unpredictable, not the kind of person you invited for Sunday lunch. He spoke of judgment, of God coming to purge the land and set the godly free. People buzzed with excitement (Luke 3:1–15).

Jesus popped up some months later, threw in his lot with the Baptist and then launched out on his own. He was very different from John. He was quieter, more sociable, and spoke of God drawing all sorts of people into his family: people who were sinners – tax-collectors, prostitutes, shepherds and the like – as well as religious folk. John had doubts about him, but, it appeared, Jesus was the one John had been sent to announce.

Jesus spent most of his ministry in Galilee. This region was about the size of Wales. The people in the prosperous, cultured south of Israel, around Jerusalem, thought it was the armpit of the world. Jesus challenged the religious élite of his day, centred on the temple and the synagogue. He said God was creating a new people, membership of which depended on how they related to Jesus, not on how much they followed the Pharisees' party line (Mark 2:22).

He was crucified in around AD 30, but God raised him from the dead. He then sent his Holy Spirit on to the small group of people who believed in him, set them on fire and sent them to turn the world upside down.

Stephen was martyred a couple of years later. Paul was probably converted within weeks of that. He got involved with the church at Antioch and set off on his first missionary journey in about AD 43. Having planted churches in Galatia, he wrote his letter to the Galatians in about 47. Following the Jerusalem Council in 48, Paul set off again, visiting Thessalonica and Philippi in 49/50 and writing 1 and 2 Thessalonians a year or two later.

While Paul was pushing into Gentile territory, Peter and James were working in Judea, and other apostles and preachers were planting churches in Samaria and Galilee. James wrote his letter to new Christians and their communities in the late 40s.

Tensions were growing between Jewish Christians and Gentile converts, so a meeting was called in 48 or 49. The Jerusalem Council, reported in Acts 15, laid down the pattern for amicable relations between Jewish and Gentile churches and set the stage for a massive expansion of the church, both geographically and numerically, in the 50s.

Through that decade, Paul and others travelled widely, preaching the gospel and planting churches in cities all over the Empire. Some of Paul's letters to churches were written in this decade (notably to Corinth and Rome) as he tried to keep the new converts on the straight and narrow, teaching them and sorting out problems. Meanwhile, Peter travelled in Asia Minor, working his way from Antioch through Corinth to Rome.

Christians didn't face official persecution at this time. Some Jews opposed Paul and made life hard for him, but the Empire was a pretty tolerant place, since there were lots of religions around. While Christians were victims of anti-

Semitism (because people saw the church as a sect within Judaism), by and large they were free to preach and teach and hold meetings. In some places they ran into trouble because their message seemed to be displacing Caesar in favour of another king (notably in Thessalonica, Acts 17:7).

Things changed towards the end of the decade and into the 60s. Emperor Nero, an unstable, paranoid, cruel man, used the Christians as scapegoats after the disastrous burning of Rome, for which he was being blamed. In a sudden explosion of ferocity against the church in the mid-60s, Paul and Peter were executed, and thousands of Christians died for no other reason than the faith they held.

While awaiting execution, Paul wrote a letter to Timothy. Peter too, and his close colleague Jude, were sending letters to the churches in Turkey in which they had worked in the early 60s.

In Israel the 60s were also a disastrous decade. Growing resentment against Roman rule exploded in a rebellion in AD 66. The Roman response was savage: Jerusalem was destroyed in AD 70 and the Jews were scattered. Following the death of James just before the rising, the Christians had left Jerusalem and settled in Pella to the East, thus avoiding the worst of the traumas that befell Israel.

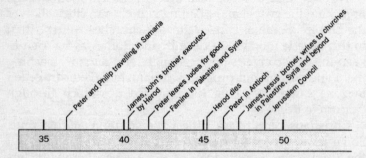

The history of the church

Into the wide blue yonder

From the 70s into the 80s the church enjoyed a respite from official persecution and continued to grow. We know very little about how it was developing. But from the letters of John, which tell us about the church around Ephesus at this time, we know that there were false teaching and leadership problems in the church, though external pressures were slight. We also know that many remained loyal to the teaching of Jesus which had been handed down by the apostles and which was now being preached by a new generation of people whose sins had been forgiven and whose lives had been turned upside down by the carpenter from Nazareth.

The peaceful years ended with the beginning of the reign of the Emperor Domitian in AD 81. He insisted on people swearing loyalty to him as a god. Failure to do so landed people in hot water.

It seems likely that the apostle John fell foul of Domitian in the mid-80s and was exiled to Patmos. In the book of Revelation, which he wrote while there, we have a searing critique of the Roman state. It is described as a beast that is out of control, persecuting the church and under the judgment of God. Revelation is also a clarion call to the

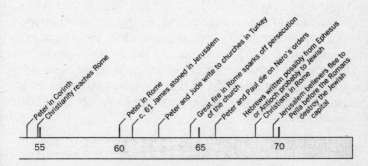

The history of the church

church to remain faithful to Jesus and to bear witness to his saving grace, even at the risk of losing liberty or life itself; for the gospel says that Jesus, not Caesar, is Lord of all.

The century closed with the church under increasing pressure. Under the Emperor Trajan (who ruled from 98 to 117), simply being a Christian seems to have been a capital offence. But many thousands had been touched and changed by the life and message of Jesus Christ. The good news of Jesus was like yeast. It was now at work in the dough of the Empire (Luke 13:20–21). Eventually, it was to take over the world that had tried so fiercely to stop it. For, although the Christians remained a persecuted minority for the next two centuries, the church grew and the message gained respect.

Finally, Constantine, almost certainly through the influence of his mother, became a Christian in the early fourth century. When he became emperor in 312, having defeated all opposition to his claim, he ascribed his victory to the God of Jesus Christ, and so Christianity became an official religion of the Empire.

The new acceptance enabled the church to sort itself out and make sure that it was remaining true to the original gospel. Various councils that met over the next fifty years or so resolved doctrinal problems and gathered the writings that everyone agreed were specially inspired by God into a collection known as the New Testament.

Since those years, as countless generations have come and gone, the gospel of Jesus Christ has remained unchanged in both its content and its power to transform people's lives. And now in our generation, this message is still turning people's lives upside down and inside out. Today there are many people who would agree with what Paul told the Christians in Rome: 'I am not ashamed of the gospel; it is the power of God to everyone who has faith' (Romans 1:16).

Caesar's world

It's commonly supposed that Christianity exploded into a single market that stretched from France to the Middle East and North Africa, in which everyone spoke the same language, and in which, under the *Pax Romana*, everyone was tied together in relative peace and prosperity.

But this is only half the picture. All through the first Christian century, the Roman world knew more than its fair share of turmoil as successive rulers sought to consolidate the Empire's hold over key strategic places and keep in check the forces of barbarism gnawing at its borders.

Roman rule was essentially pragmatic by nature and so tended to be handled by a patchwork of different kinds of officials. In some places local client rulers were the order of the day. Herod and his family were one such local dynasty entrusted to keep the peace. In other places, provincial governors were responsible for handling tax revenues (set centrally but gathered locally by universally unpopular tax farmers), hearing legal cases and deploying the military if needed (usually in some policing capacity to quell disorder). These were the people granted the 'power of the sword' by the Roman senate (cf. Romans 13:4).

In difficult-to-manage places, imperial legates were placed directly by the emperor. One such legate was Quirinius (Luke 2:1–2; Acts 5:37). They had wide-ranging powers to keep the peace and impose the *Pax Romana*, by force if necessary. Other regions were ruled by prefects or procurators, such as Pontius Pilate in Palestine. And some parts of the Empire were overseen by praetors or consuls, appointed by the Roman senate as a reward for services rendered to Rome. We come across many of these in Acts: Sergius Paulus in Cyprus (13:7), Gallio in Achaia (18:12), and the unnamed consul of Ephesus (19:38).

All this explains why we encounter a variety of responses to Christian activity in Acts. Different officials applied the rules differently and had different powers according to their status and place in the Roman pecking order. They also took varying lines on Christian activity, some adopting a 'live and let live' policy providing the public order was maintained, others using the law to curtail activities they disapproved of. Only later in the century did the law seem to harden against Christian practice and mission.

Travel within the Empire was relatively easy. Movement on land was mainly by foot, though the rich might use horses or horse-drawn carriages of some kind. The roads were generally safe (for the legions had freed them of bandits in the heart of the Empire) and teeming with traders *en route* between the major commercial centres of the Empire. It was along these trade routes that the early missionaries travelled, sharing the good news as they went.

Sea travel was also safe, and plenty of ships plied the routes from Italy to the eastern Mediterranean carrying goods and people to countless thriving port cities. The major hazards at sea were the weather and poor seamanship rather than pirates.

The language of the Empire – thanks to the conquests of Alexander the Great rather than any Caesar – was Greek. The further west you travelled, the less well it was spoken. But there's plenty of evidence of Greek-speakers in first-century Britain, indicating that it was the *lingua franca* of all trade, commerce and political discourse in the Empire. This was a huge boon to the outreach of the church. It meant that missionaries could communicate in the same language to everyone they met.

Books and writing flourished in the peace and security of the Empire. Literacy rates were low overall, but among the merchants and officials of the Empire, reading was both essential and popular. Many poets and philosophers saw their work published around the Empire, so it's not surprising that the Christians put their story in writing fairly early on. And, of course, Paul kept in touch with his growing network of churches through letters, as did the other travelling apostles.

The first-century smorgasbord of beliefs

Christianity was born in a world awash with gods. Although Judea was firmly monotheistic, the rest of the Empire swarmed with religions, philosophies and beliefs of every conceivable type. Even Galilee had more than its fair share of pagan temples and shrines, a legacy of hundreds of years of Graeco-Roman influence. So Jesus and the early Christians proclaimed their message of God's coming rule to people sated with metaphysical ideas.

Pick a god, any god ...

As the Roman Empire supplanted Alexander's Greek Empire, so their gods mingled with the gods of the Greeks. There was a particular identification between the key Roman deities (Jupiter, Juno, Minerva, Venus, Mercury, Mars, Neptune) and the Greek pantheon (Zeus, Hera, Poseidon, Hades, Apollo, Artemis, Athena, Aphrodite, Hermes, Dionysus). But Greek and Roman styles of worship were different. So religion in the west of the Empire differed from that in the more Hellenistic east.

The Greek world had comprised hundreds of fiercely independent city states, each with its own deity or individual take on a deity from the pantheon. The cities had many temples and everyone participated in the public ceremonies that ensured that the gods would look favourably on them.

The Roman world sought peace with the gods in the *pax deorum* (a sort of spiritual equivalent of the *Pax Romana* that held the Empire together). All disasters that befell the Empire were blamed on breaches of the *pax* by human disrespect for the divine order, and especially by irregular or new forms of worship. Public ceremonies, during which sacrifices were made and prayers offered, were important occasions which all citizens were expected to participate in.

In both the Hellenistic and Roman parts of the Empire, these ceremonies were formal civic affairs. To participate in them, you didn't have to believe that the deity was particularly interested in your town, or even that the deity actually existed. So those looking for a genuine religious experience turned to the plethora of mystery cults. These were often associated with particular places or trades or social classes or cohorts in the legion. They consisted of initiation rituals – often involving a 'baptism' of some kind – and regular offering of sacrifices, oblations and prayers in order to ensure that the cult god would look favourably on you.

The mystery cults gave their adherents a sense of belonging often absent from the more formal religious activities. They also promised access to divine power and immortality. They offered personal rather than civic salvation. So they were very popular.

All religion in this world was sensual, with ceremonies often accompanied by sexual acts on the part of the priests and worshippers. Evidence from Pompeii, for instance, indicates that graphic depictions of sexual activity were commonplace, and that sex played a central role in many religious ceremonies.

Following the leader

All over the Empire the imperial cult gained ground throughout the first century. It had begun when the Roman senate deified Julius Caesar after his death, and suggested that his adopted son Augustus was also divine. People began to offer incense and prayers to the emperor, especially in the eastern Empire, where worship of great leaders of the past was an established practice.

To begin with, the imperial cult honoured dead Caesars, but it wasn't long before living ones saw the benefit of being treated like a god. By the time of Domitian in the 80s, worshipping the emperor was official policy; everyone had to do it on pain of severe punishment (as the apostle John found out).

The imperial cult titled Caesar both *sōtēr* and *kyrios* (saviour and lord), terms the Christians used exclusively of Jesus. From Augustus onwards, Caesar was also known as 'son of god', because Augustus was the deified Julius Caesar's son. Christian usage of this term applied to Jesus is derived, not from this practice, but from the Old Testament designation of Israel's kings as sons of Yahweh. But, of course, referring to a rival king as Son of God would naturally land Christians in hot water with the authorities, who were at pains to stress that divine Caesar was son of god, saviour and lord and that no-one else had the right to claim those titles.

Pausing for thought

Many found what was on offer absolutely to their taste. But others didn't. There's evidence that by the first century there was a growing disenchantment with religion of all kinds. This was leading to renewed interest in philosophy and ideas.

It needs to be stressed that most philosophers of this age were not atheists, and people meeting to talk about the latest theories might go on from there to worship in a public temple or private mystery cult. But there certainly was an interest in ways of seeing the world different from those offered by the religious hierarchies..

The *Epicureans*, for instance, though believing in the gods, thought religion irrelevant to life. They believed that everything could be explained through the interaction of natural forces, and believed strongly in free will. The purpose of their ideas was to free people from superstition and fear. Life was for living and to be enjoyed, and hence they got a bit of a reputation for being profligate and effeminate.

The *Stoics*, by contrast, sought to live lives of reverence, believing all things to be god. Their key concern was how we might live an ethical life in harmony with the natural order; and that differed from person to person. So Stoicism was a fiercely individualistic creed and one characterized by asceticism. Unlike the Epicureans, the Stoics didn't party.

The *Cynics*, who pre-dated and gave rise to the Stoics, also believed that life should be lived according to nature. For the Cynics, this meant lives of the utmost simplicity. Their founder, Diogenes, lived in a barrel, with only a cloak and cup to his name. Eventually he even gave up the cup. Cynics rejected social norms and lived as wandering beggars, uttering aphorisms that many regarded as wise and others as nonsense.

Other schools also blossomed, and in many cities (as Paul discovered in Athens) there were lively debating-groups eager to discuss the latest ideas and find the key to the good life everyone wanted.

The second founder:
the life and travels of Paul

In the sharp sunlight, he was standing guard over a pile of coats, sternly nodding his approval. A group of men, their faces masked by shadows from the nearby city wall, were hurling stones, boulders, or any lump of masonry they could lift, at the bleeding form of a man dying out in the merciless heat. The group finished their bloody toil, gathered their coats and melted away into the hustle of the city streets. Their anger spent on the church's first martyr, Stephen, they went back to their daily routines (Acts 7:54 – 8:1).

But for Saul, the young rabbi who had guarded their coats, it was only the beginning. If Stephen could be removed, then so could all the other 'heretics', all those who preached that Jesus from Nazareth, a trouble-maker crucified a couple of years before, was God's Messiah.

A few days later, having set off from Jerusalem to Damascus on a mission to destroy the church there, Saul was preaching that Jesus was the Messiah, the Lord of all. So powerful was his preaching, so radical the change in him, so effective his call to Jews to believe in Jesus, that a plot to kill him was hatched. He had to escape from Damascus in a basket.

For the next twenty-five to thirty years Saul, better known by his Greek name Paul, planted churches in every major city of the eastern Roman Empire, wrote letters (thirteen of which form the heart of the New Testament) and had an impact that earned him the title 'the second founder of Christianity'.

The man for the Gentiles

Paul once told a Roman officer at Jerusalem, 'I am a Jew, from Tarsus in Cilicia, a citizen of an important city' (Acts 21:39). Tarsus, on the Turkish coast, on a main east–west trade route, was a centre of the textile industry. Paul was born into a wealthy family in this prosperous city. His father must have done some great service to Rome, because Paul was born a Roman citizen. Perhaps his father had supplied tents or leather goods to the Roman army.

Citizenship made Paul part of the social élite. That and his family's undoubted wealth meant that he had access to the very best in education. Tarsus was a centre of culture and learning, philosophy and art. Paul clearly made the most of it, as can be seen from his ability to write, to argue a case and to quote freely and extensively from Greek and Roman ideas and literature.

A man with a mission

For all his wealth, learning and social status, what mattered most to Paul was that he was a Jew. As he told the Philippian Christians, he was 'circumcised on the eighth day, a member of the people of Israel, of the tribe of Benjamin, a Hebrew born of Hebrews; as to the law, a Pharisee' (Philippians 3:5).

He came from a strict Jewish home, where Aramaic was probably spoken. He would have attended the local synagogue school, where he would have been tutored in the law and the tradition of his people. Then he went to Jerusalem to finish his education. Going to Jerusalem was pretty impressive for a boy from the Diaspora, but to sit at the feet of the great Gamaliel was something else. Paul got the very best Jewish education that money and connections could secure (Acts 22:3).

But he was always more than just a well-educated rabbi.

He had fire in his belly. He belonged to the Shammaite school (see chapter 15). From his career in Acts and the tone and content of his letters, it is clear that Paul was never an ivory-tower theologian or bookish academic. He was passionate about everything he did; he did it all for a purpose and saw himself as a man with a mission.

This commitment and drive are seen before his conversion to Christianity. While still a pupil (though probably nearing the end of his studies, which makes him around thirty years old), he began to oppose the young church. He did not just engage the Christians in debate; he wanted to snuff out the movement. Hence his role in Stephen's martyrdom.

Here we see the difference between Paul and his distinguished teacher. Gamaliel, from the Hillelite faction of Pharisaism, clearly wanted to reserve judgment on Christianity. When the apostles were arrested and brought before the court in Jerusalem, it was Gamaliel who counselled caution, saying that if the movement was just a human phenomenon it would fail, as other such movements had before it; but if it was a move of God within Judaism, the leaders of the Jews would not be able to stop it. Worse, to try to stop it would be tantamount to fighting God (Acts 5:34–40).

Gamaliel's 'wait and see' wisdom prevailed, and the apostles were released. But Paul wasn't so patient. The new heresy had to be stamped out. God needed a helping hand, and Paul, the passionate Shammaite, was just the man to offer it. Having seen off Stephen and having helped to spark off widespread persecution of the church in Jerusalem, he played a prominent part in arresting known Christians. So effective was his assault on the believers that many of them fled the city. Paul, scenting victory, and having caught the public mood, was empowered by the priests in Jerusalem to spread the net wider. He set off to Damascus, pledged to weed out the Christians before the church could take root there.

Blinded by the light

In the heat and dust of the Damascus road Paul ran into the person he was least expecting – Jesus. The meeting rocked Paul to the core, shattered his old understanding of God and the world, and planted the seeds that blossomed into his radical gospel of freedom (Acts 9:1–19).

Within sight of the walls of Damascus, Paul met the living Jesus. So Jesus wasn't the rightly crucified messianic pretender that Paul had thought. If God had raised him from the dead, then his claim to be the bringer of the kingdom, the source of new life, and the one who would give the Holy Spirit to his followers and usher in the new age, must be true.

But there was more. If Jesus was the Messiah and he had ended up on a cross, that can't have been an accident. God would not have allowed his plans for his Messiah to be thwarted by chance. So the cross must have been central to Jesus' work as the Messiah, and central in the defeat of Israel's enemies and the establishment of God's kingdom.

And surely there was still more. The glorious appearance of Jesus on the road was very like the glorious appearance of God when he showed himself to people in Old Testament times. What did this tell Paul, blinded by that light, his mind sent into a whirl of speculation, about who and what Jesus was?

And finally, why did Jesus say that Paul was persecuting *him*, when he was in fact persecuting the church? What did this begin to teach Paul about the nature of the church as the body of Christ on earth?

All these questions and implications arose from Paul's encounter with Jesus on the road. But, as ever with Paul, he did not withdraw for the luxury of several months' quiet reflection on these issues while he got together a perfect systematic theology with which he could wow the world. Paul hardly paused to catch his breath.

This little light of mine

He was led into Damascus, helpless and blind. He was met by Ananias, who was none too pleased at the prospect and took some persuading from God before he went. He baptized Paul and welcomed him into the fellowship of the church. The rather stunned believers met the new convert and listened to him powerfully proclaiming the risen Jesus to Jews in the city. This latter activity (which could well have lasted up to three years, depending on how we relate Acts 9 to Galatians 1) did not go down well with Paul's former supporters. They plotted his death, and he had to escape (Acts 9:19–22).

He came to Jerusalem at around this time and met the apostles who were still there. It has to be said that they were suspicious of him; but Barnabas took him under his wing, introduced him to everyone and gave him the opportunity to preach and teach. The situation in Jerusalem was delicate, and Paul's style stirred up vicious opposition among the religious and political authorities. It was time to move on again.

Paul left Jerusalem for Tarsus, his home town. We know nothing of his stay there, though it is probably fair to speculate that he would have had some difficulty explaining his conversion to his family. Life would not have been easy for this promising son who kicked over the traces and threw in his lot with a new and, in the eyes of his father and his former teachers, dangerously heretical sect.

Barnabas came and found him some time later and took him to a new church in Antioch, mid-way between Tarsus and Damascus. Jewish Christians who had been scattered by the persecution that had broken out after Stephen was martyred had worked their way up to Antioch, the commercial and political capital of the Roman province of Syria. They preached wherever they went to whoever would listen, and for the first time Gentiles came into the church (Acts 11:25–26).

This mixed church needed teaching and setting on a firm foundation. Barnabas could think of no better colleague for this work than Paul, the one Jesus had called to be his messenger to the Gentiles.

From Antioch Paul and Barnabas were sent as the church's first missionaries to Asia Minor. On their return home, they ran into trouble with those who said that Gentiles had to become Jews in order to be Christians, which probably resulted in Paul writing to the churches he'd just planted in Galatia. Then Paul and Barnabas went to Jerusalem for a crucial meeting of the apostles to talk about evangelism among the Gentiles. Paul seems to have been fairly pleased with the outcome: that Gentiles didn't have to become Jews to become Christians.

Have mission, will travel

For much of the next ten years he travelled, preaching the good news of Jesus and planting churches. He never travelled alone. From his letters it is clear that there was always a team around him. Sometimes, if Paul was staying a long time in one place (for instance, he spent eighteen months at Ephesus), members of his team would go to the outlying towns and villages and preach the gospel there. For example, while Paul was at Ephesus, Epaphras planted the church at Colosse just down the valley (Acts 19:1–10).

As well as preaching, Paul also raised funds, not for himself, but for the poor in the church at Jerusalem and in Judea. Through the 40s and 50s, life in Israel was bleak. Famine and economic hardship meant that many Christians had virtually nothing to live on. Paul could not stand by and do nothing about this tragedy.

So he appealed to the Gentile churches he had founded – and to some he hadn't – to help relieve the poverty of the Jewish congregations in Palestine. As well as bringing practical aid to the suffering Christians, Paul also believed that this would demonstrate the unity of the church and the reality of the fellowship of believers in Christ. And furthermore, he felt that this offering by Gentile Christians would somehow demonstrate the truth of the gospel to his own people, the Jews. It is this collection that Paul is talking about in 1 Corinthians 16:1–4 and 2 Corinthians 9.

In around 57 he brought the collection to Jerusalem. He had been warned that his journey would be dangerous (Acts 21:17), but he wanted to bring the offering personally. Having done so, he was arrested in the temple and brought before the Council. They wanted to execute him, but couldn't without Roman approval; and because Paul was a Roman citizen he couldn't be treated in the summary way that Jesus was (Acts 21:27 – 23:22).

The Roman governor, who had been warned that certain people, with the approval of the priests, were planning to kill Paul on his next public appearance, had him moved under armed guard to the safe-keeping of Governor Felix in Caesarea. Felix couldn't decide what to do with the troublesome missionary, and Paul remained in prison for two years (Acts 23:23 – 24:27).

Felix was replaced by Festus (Acts 25:1–32), and he, keen to curry favour with the Jewish leaders in Jerusalem, wanted to send Paul back there for trial. So Paul appealed to Caesar, as it was the right of every Roman citizen to be tried personally by the emperor. After a hazardous and eventful journey (Acts 27:1 – 28:10), Paul arrived in Rome. There he remained for two years, able to preach and teach and receive visitors, awaiting his trial (Acts 28:11–31).

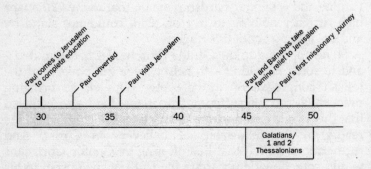

Paul's travels and letters

A final spurt

This much we know from Acts. But that's where Luke leaves off. And we aren't sure what happened next. It seems likely that some time after the end of Acts, Paul was released. He travelled again, possibly to Spain, as he had told the Roman church he wanted to. He then probably went back to Corinth, which served as the hub of a new work around Turkey and the Aegean – including sorting out a mess in the church at Ephesus and planting a church in Crete. It was probably during this time that Paul wrote 1 Timothy and Titus, which refer to those two situations.

It is quite likely that he was there for two years or so, from about 64 to 66. Towards the end of this time, the church in Rome began to suffer appallingly at the hands of Nero. Peter had probably already died at the hands of this madman. At great personal risk, Paul went to Rome in about 66 or 67 to strengthen and encourage the Roman Christians. There he met his death after composing a last, poignant letter to his dear friend and colleague Timothy.

Words on the run

When I was a young Christian I was asked to give my

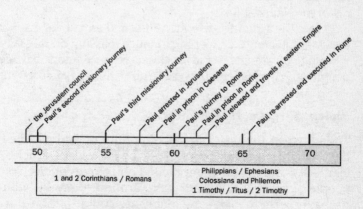

Paul's travels and letters

187

testimony at a school meeting. I was scared witless! But I was encouraged by a letter from Dave Pope. At that time he was an evangelist with the Movement for World Evangelization and was about to release his first album. He and I had never met; he knew about me through one of his colleagues.

He wrote that he was thrilled to hear that I'd become a Christian and was about to tell others what Jesus meant to me. He assured me that God would give me the courage I needed to take this step and that he'd be praying for me. I was knocked for six. It was such an encouragement that someone like Dave Pope should take an interest in me. Letters can give people's faith such a boost. Perhaps the Christians in Philippi and Thessalonica felt that way when a letter from Paul arrived.

But there are also other kinds of letters that we're not so keen to receive. I got a letter once from a couple involved in youth work at the church I was attending at the time, telling me how hurt they had been by something I had done. The letter warned me that our friendship was at risk if I didn't do something. I felt a mixture of anger and sorrow, but I knew I had to act. The issue between us was resolved, I was forgiven, and our relationship was restored. I guess I felt a bit of what the Corinthian Christians must have felt during their correspondence with Paul – a correspondence which was long and painful, but which, it seems, ultimately resulted in restored relationships.

Before the age of the telephone, fax and e-mail, letters were the essential means of keeping in touch, passing on messages, warning of dangers and seeking reconciliation between people who had fallen out. We see all of this in Paul's letters.

'Quick, Silvanus, take a letter'

Today, when the major issues of politics or faith are being debated or promoted, people write books, essays, articles in learned journals and pamphlets. Paul wrote letters. Some people suggest that if Paul were around today he would probably write books – if a publisher could tie him down long enough to meet a deadline! Paul did live in a time when people wrote books. At Alexandria in Egypt there lived a devout Jew who committed his life to proving to the Gentile world that the Jewish understanding of things was the right one. His name was Philo, and he wrote books – books with a beginning, a middle and an end, books with a line of argument that could be followed quite easily by anyone picking them up.

Paul, however, chose to write letters. He had been called by God to preach the good news of Jesus to the Gentiles, and he did this by planting churches in key urban centres. Having started a church, he would stay a while to ensure that the church's foundations were strong and that leaders were in place, and then he would move on. He kept in touch with the churches he founded by making visits and by writing letters.

The nature of Paul's life meant that he wrote only when he heard of a major problem in a church (Galatians, 1 and 2 Corinthians); or when he was in prison (Philippians), the forced leisure time being put to good pastoral use; or when he was asked questions (1 Corinthians, 1 Thessalonians). He frequently had to defend himself against attacks made on his character or ministry by other 'apostles' (1 and 2 Corinthians, 1 Thessalonians). He also wrote to individual members of his ministry team who had been given a specific job to do. He wrote to encourage them – as Dave Pope did to me – and to remind them of what they should be doing (1 and 2 Timothy, Titus).

Paul's letters were always provoked by something happening in the church he was writing to. He never seems have sat down and said to himself: 'I know, I'll drop a note to the church at Damascus, telling them all about the doctrine of justification by faith.' He wrote in response to a crisis or false teaching or some situation that might affect the long-term health of the church in question.

Reading Paul's letters is a bit like hearing one end of a phone conversation. We rarely know what the specific event was that provoked Paul to put pen to parchment, or to get his secretary to take a letter. We have to try to work it out from what he said.

Paul's teaching comes to us, not in a systematic and carefully ordered way, but as arguments used to persuade his readers that he and not his opponents had the right understanding of the Christian faith.

The view from the battlefield

Paul was no ivory-tower theologian watching the world and the church from the wings, but a working minister and evangelist who lived in the thick of the battle to establish the church of Jesus Christ.

But his letters are not random jottings or haphazard missives fired off in a rush between engagements. He wrote with care, and there is a sharp and creative mind behind what he wrote, even though the occasion for each of his letters was a problem in or a request from a church. The letters exploded out of his rich intellect and fertile imagination. To understand the letters, you need understand the man and his sense of calling.

Paul was first and foremost a pastor. He cared deeply and passionately for the people he had led to the Lord and the churches he had founded. He was anxious when he heard that congregations were troubled by persecution, divisions or false teaching (Colossians 1 – 2).

Sometimes he wrote to answer specific questions raised by churches (1 Corinthians, 1 Thessalonians); sometimes because he had heard of serious problems in a church from a close friend or colleague (Colossians, Galatians); and sometimes because he knew that a friend needed encouragement (1 Timothy).

Paul is often seen as a cold, fierce, rigid dogmatist. But this is an awful caricature. He sometimes pastored in anger, but usually he spoke with great gentleness. We see this in his fatherly concern for the Thessalonians, his anguish over Titus' health, his yearning to see Philemon and Onesimus reconciled, and his longing for companionship when he faced danger. His great heart for people is seen in the long list of greetings in Romans 16.

Secondly, Paul was a teacher. His message was derived

from Jesus Christ himself, whom he had met on the road to Damascus, and from the teaching of the church handed down from the very beginning. He taught this truth winsomely, with great conviction, angrily and gently (compare and contrast two early letters written within a couple of years of each other: Galatians and 1 Thessalonians).

His teaching had two major purposes. The first was to refute false teaching and to correct people's misunderstandings. When he heard that Christians in Galatia were getting circumcised and were trying to keep the Jewish law, he wrote furiously, denouncing the people who were laying such burdens on the young believers and passionately defending his gospel of faith and freedom (Galatians 3:1; Colossians 2:4).

His teaching in 1 Corinthians 12 – 14 is not a measured summary of everything there is to know about spiritual gifts, but an attempt to correct false views about the importance of tongues and to prevent the Corinthians' worship from descending into chaos.

His second purpose was to remind people of the central truths of the faith, and especially that they must live the Christian life in a way that shows the world that the gospel is true. So he stresses that people can be right with God only through faith in Jesus. But, once put right, our lives should be marked by good works, kind words and a lifestyle that honours God.

Building on the past

Thirdly, Paul was a Pharisee. This meant that his whole way of thinking had been shaped by the Old Testament and the teaching of the synagogue. When he met Jesus on the road to Damascus he didn't ditch this rich heritage; he wasn't spirited away from his past. He wrestled with how to interpret his Bible (the Old Testament) in the light of the experience of meeting the risen Jesus. And so his teaching is rooted in the Scriptures he had grown up with (Philippians 3:4–5).

As he studied and prayed, he saw that God had always accepted people on the basis of their faith (Romans 4), and that the things that marked the Jews out from the world – circumcision, the Sabbath, certain rules regarding what you eat and how you eat it – had been fine in their day as an outward expression of that faith. But now they had been superseded by Christ and the coming of the Holy Spirit. What marked out the people of God now was not these so-called 'works of the law' but the fruit of the Holy Spirit, made possible by faith in Christ.

Paul frequently refers to and quotes from the Old Testament. When he does so, he shows how a particular passage is fulfilled in Jesus, and how it now applies to those who are members of God's people through faith in Jesus (1 Corinthians 10:6).

His passion for the Old Testament is seen most clearly in his letter to the church at Rome. It was written during a three-month pause in around AD 56, and many see it as his finest work. Many also suggest that Romans is less a letter and more a treatise, a summation of his gospel, possibly written to elicit Rome's support for his proposed missionary travels to Spain.

But even Romans was written with an eye on the church it was going to. Paul's magisterial defence of the truth that God accepts people, not on the basis of their birth and breeding, but on the basis of their faith in Christ, was written to a church where there were tensions between Jews and Gentiles. At that time Paul's whole emphasis was under attack from other Christians – so-called 'Judaizers' – who felt that the gospel required all believers, Jews and Gentiles, to keep the Old Testament law at least in some respects.

This is why Paul spends so much time talking about the Day of Atonement, Abraham, Adam, the law, the relationship between Israel and the church, and how all these are affected by the coming of Jesus. It all leads up to Romans 15:7, where he appeals to us to 'welcome one another, therefore, just as Christ has welcomed you, for the glory of God'.

As a Pharisee he would also have had an apocalyptic

outlook, a way of viewing the world and God's activity in it informed by the writings of apocalyptic visionaries as well as the Old Testament prophets (see chapter 16). Evidence of this outlook can be seen in Paul's understanding that the kingdom of God came in Jesus, and especially in his view that though the age of the kingdom had started in Jesus, it wouldn't come in all its fullness until Jesus came to reign in glory. It is also apparent in his theology of the Spirit, which sees the Spirit as the bringer of the fruits of the life of the kingdom (see Galatians 5 – 6; 1 Corinthians 15).

'Do as I say and as I do'

Finally, Paul wrote as an apostle. As the opening of Galatians makes abundantly clear, Paul had no doubts about his calling or his gospel: both came straight from God. In 1 Corinthians he stresses that what he teaches is inspired by the Spirit and should be obeyed. He is so certain that the message upon which he has based his life and ministry is the whole truth that he can appeal to his readers to copy his lifestyle; if they do that, they'll be copying Christ (1 Corinthians 11:1).

In anyone else this would have been appalling arrogance. Yet even in his lifetime others sensed that some of what Paul wrote was special in the way the Old Testament Scriptures were special. Not everything, though. Paul wrote more than the thirteen letters collected in the New Testament. These thirteen writings were seen to be especially touched by God, unlike the two lost letters he wrote to Corinth, or the letter he wrote to the Laodiceans, or his other letters, of which we know nothing. By the end of the first century, his letters were being used as Scripture, as the authoritative Word of God, in churches all over the Middle East. (2 Peter 3:16 indicates that even earlier than the end of the century, Paul's letters were being put alongside 'other scriptures' and treated accordingly.)

Catching the drift

When we come to a passage in one of Paul's letters, our first question should not be, 'What's this saying to me?' We need first of all to remind ourselves who the letter was written to, why Paul wrote it (to challenge and correct false teaching, or to answer questions, or to give more detail to teaching already touched on), and where the passage we're reading comes in the flow of his argument. We need to note whether he is quoting the Old Testament, and if so, what he's quoting and how he's using it.

Taking Colossians 2:6–15 as an example, how does this work? This passage urges us to stay rooted in Christ (verses 6–7), to resist the world (verse 8) and to receive the fullness which is found only in Jesus (verses 9–15). The language Paul uses is rather odd, however: he talks of fullness, refers (apparently out of the blue) to circumcision and baptism, and mentions spiritual powers and authorities. This should alert us to the fact that Paul was probably countering some kind of false teaching that emphasized these things.

Sure enough, a little background reading reveals that the Colossian church was troubled by teachers who talked a lot about needing to add new experiences to their faith in Jesus in order to receive the fullness of God their lives. These teachers stressed the need to acquire secret knowledge – things that ordinary Christians didn't know – if you wanted to be especially spiritual. They said that it was necessary to go through secret initiation rituals to get a leg up on to a higher plane of Christian living.

Paul counters this teaching by stressing that the fullness of God is found only in Jesus. He had gone into detail about this in Colossians 1, where he had composed or quoted a wonderful poetic hymn of praise to Christ, the church's Lord, the visible image of the unseen God (verses 15–20). He goes on to say that we experience the fullness of God through faith in Christ's death on the cross. It is his death on our behalf that has dealt with our sin and with all the oppressive powers, human and divine, that would prevent us from enjoying the fullness of life God wants us to have.

Far from needing to undergo some secret ritual, through our baptism we have already testified to our faith in Jesus and begun to enjoy all the things which that faith has opened up to us. That's all we need, says Paul, because the way to fullness of life is through faith in Jesus, not secret knowledge and flashy new experiences, however wonderful and plausible they sound.

We need to do this kind of exercise every time we read a passage in one of Paul's letters. In this way we'll catch his drift and not get caught in some whirlpool of misunderstanding that does no justice to Paul and nothing to build up our faith.

21

Going to church in the first century

Many Christian groups talk confidently about how their way of doing things accords with New Testament practice. This is amazing, given how little we know about what going to church in first-century Corinth or Nazareth was actually like. What time were the services? How often did Christians meet together? What sort of liturgy did the churches employ? Who led the worship? How many people attended the average meeting? If only we knew!

What is clear from the New Testament, and what archaeology has been able to confirm, is that for the first three centuries Christians did not put up special buildings to house their activities. When Paul wrote to churches, his letter went to a private address on an ordinary street in whatever city he was writing to. Often he greeted churches that met in various people's homes (Romans 16:3–4, 10, 11, 14, 15) and sent greetings from similar churches (Romans 16:16b, where 'all the churches' is probably a reference to all the small house churches that met in Corinth, where the letter was written from).

This means that the average church congregation was small, probably no more than thirty to forty. After all, how many people could you get in the average first-century family home? Even the villas of the well-off were limited in the amount of space they had, and there is good evidence, as we'll see in a minute, that a majority of believers at this time were from the lower orders of society and hence might not have had access to spacious accommodation.

Only in Acts is there evidence that Christians met somewhere other than in people's homes. Luke tells us that the early believers met in houses around Jerusalem (Acts 2:46b), but he also points out that they met in the temple courts (2:46a). This was a big space, able to accommodate very large numbers of people – though probably not three thousand at a time.

It's clear that much of the action Luke records in the early chapters of Acts took place in and around the temple area. This is because the new Jesus movement was still very much a sect within Judaism rather than a separate religion. It was also because, in terms of church order, Peter and the other leaders were making it up as they went along. All they had to go on was their Jewish synagogue background and their experience of being with Jesus. Nearly everything Jesus had done happened either in public or at parties in people's homes. (Look at Luke's Gospel to see the importance to Jesus of meal tables as a venue for teaching; see *Discovering Luke's Gospel*, p. 184.)

The very early church followed suit. They milled about the temple courts talking about what happened on the first Christian Pentecost and recalling the teaching of Jesus. People came and went freely from the group, with intrigued onlookers wondering whether to stick around and find out more. These early believers were held in high regard, especially after a miraculous healing at the temple gate and a run-in with the ever unpopular Sadducean authorities (Acts 3 – 4). The people weren't so sure when two believers were carried dead from the temple gathering of this new sect (Acts 5:1–11)! At that point Luke tells us that the church kept meeting in Solomon's Portico in the temple, where they were held in high but circumspect regard (5:12–16).

It seems that what happened in public was mainly the proclamation of the good news about Jesus, with the apostles explaining what had occurred to start this new renewal movement within Judaism. This remained the practice of the church as it spread into Gentile territory, especially through the journeys of Paul. When Paul arrived in a town, he went to synagogues and market-places where he could proclaim the good news to both Jews and Gentiles. He even sought out places where people exchanged ideas and talked about the meaning of life over a flagon or two of wine (see Acts 17:16–34).

Once people had come to faith, homes, or, in a few rare instances, hired halls, were the normal meeting-places for fellowship, teaching and prayer. Meals played an important part in early Christian gatherings. To begin with, these meals were just that, occasions for eating – though no doubt as they broke bread and shared wine (the hallmarks of any meal in the ancient world) they also remembered the cross of their Lord.

And the fact that Christians met to eat together could give a hint as to the timings of their gatherings. They had to meet outside working hours (pretty much sunrise to sunset), as they would not be able to take time off to practise their new religion. So this leaves breakfast and dinner-time as the likely times that Christians met in each other's homes. There is evidence from the catacombs in Rome that the church gathered there early in the morning – though this is second-century evidence.

As they gathered, as well as eating and, through that, remembering the cross of Christ, they also prayed for one another and received teaching and shared in mutual encouragement. 1 Corinthians 14 contains teaching on what normal church gatherings should be like, and it's clear from there that Paul expected people to find it a helpful time when they could be built up in their faith, so that when they were at work or at home, among people who didn't follow Jesus, their lives would speak of the reality of their faith. It's also worth noting that Paul expects such times to be intelligible to outsiders (14:24–25).

The salt of the earth

There is plenty of evidence that the bulk of people who became Christians in the first century were from the lower social orders (1 Corinthians 1:26). An examination of the

Roman house churches (see *Discovering Romans*, p. 224) reveals that three of the five house churches identified in Romans 16 comprised slaves and poor labourers.

This was probably the norm throughout the Empire. The Christian message of new life, coupled with the Christian practice of economic sharing, made it particularly attractive to the poor. Those with a stake in the current social order, who benefited economically and socially from the *status quo*, were less likely to get involved with a Jewish sect whose founder had been crucified by the Romans.

This meant that churches were probably led by the few heads of households who converted to the new faith. The owners of houses large enough to host a Christian gathering, and who were already used to exercising leadership as heads of extended households, with numbers of slaves, lands and enterprises to manage, probably took the lead in their congregations. These people were also the few in any congregation who had the literacy skills necessary to read correspondence from apostles or the Scriptures (the Old Testament), which some might have had in book form. Philemon, a man of means, who had a congregation meeting in his house, was one such leader; as was Phoebe, who appears to have been leader of a congregation in Cenchrae as well as the main funder of Paul's intended mission to Spain.

This undoubtedly explains why so much teaching in the letters is devoted to what scholars have called 'the household codes'. This teaching, found in Colossians 3, Ephesians 4 – 5, and 1 Peter 3 among other places, focuses on how Christians should relate to each other in the typical Graeco-Roman extended household. Such households would have consisted of members of the extended family, slaves and others who all lived and worked together. It was vital that these units should function in a Christian way, especially as the heads of the household were often leading the church and so had to be examples of godly conduct. It also explains why one of Paul's favourite pictures of the church is the household (see Ephesians 2:11–22).

When the Christians gathered, everyone appears to have

had a role in worship. There is evidence from the language used to describe Christian gatherings and behaviour in the New Testament that the focus of Christian meetings was on mutual edification. There is very little stress on what is traditionally thought of as worship: singing, offering sacrifices (unnecessary because of the cross), and reciting creeds and confessions. Rather, the focus is on prayer and teaching, on bringing needs to God and on hearing God respond through Bible exposition and prophecy. Hence everyone could have a role in building up everyone else, though it clear from the very earliest days that some had particular teaching and leading roles that were respected by the others. When that respect broke down, churches got into trouble, as we see all too graphically in Paul's letters to the Corinthian congregations.

Getting a hard time

It wasn't easy going to church in the first century. From the word 'Go', Christians got a hard time for following Jesus. It's easy to see why this might have been the case in Jewish circles: after all, Jesus had challenged the emerging orthodox Judaism of his day, and Acts tells us that the temple authorities tried to stamp out the new movement. It is less certain why the usually tolerant Romans and Greeks of the Gentile world gave Christians a hard time.

By the end of the first century, merely admitting to being a Christian seems to have been enough to get you executed. Correspondence between the Emperor Trajan and his governor in Bythinia, Pliny, indicates that this was normal practice, though Trajan stresses that there should be no general witch-hunt against Christians. This suggests that if believers kept their heads down, they wouldn't get them lopped off.

It seems that opposition to Christians among the Gentile citizens of the Empire grew through the first century for two reasons.

First, Christianity was seen as an off-shoot of Judaism. And while the faith of Israel was officially tolerated because of Israel's support of Rome against the Selucids, at the eastern end of the Empire that support caused animosity between Hellenistic people and Jews. By the first century, even the Romans were having second thoughts, because Palestine was beginning to be a thorn in the Empire's side.

There were frequent pogroms in various parts of the empire between 50 BC and AD 150. In the late 40s, the Jews were expelled from Rome, possibly because of in-fighting in the Jewish community over whether Jesus was the Messiah or not. Thousands of Jews were massacred in Antioch in AD 67 because they were blamed for trying to set the city on fire – something Nero had accused Christians of doing in Rome three years earlier.

All this made Christians a target in some towns and cities. It made Christians susceptible to casual and random acts of racist violence in their neighbourhoods.

But secondly, something about Christianity itself repelled cultivated and loyal Roman citizens. Suetonius described Christianity as a 'mischievous superstition', Tacitus says that Christians were 'loathed for their vices', and Pliny depicted Christianity as a 'depraved and excessive superstition'. How could these otherwise intelligent and urbane men have come to such a conclusion?

The most plausible suggestion is that, because the Christians had no official meeting place (no temple or synagogue), but rather met in secret in people's homes, they must have had something to hide. This, coupled with the fact that they refused to join in the growing cult of emperor worship, caused the infant church to be seen as a potential threat to the state.

Rumours of what these people did in their private gatherings suggested that the Christian movement conformed to a stereotype of the conspiratorial group hell-bent on destroying the Roman Empire. Like the Bacchanalia, the Cataline and Torquinian movements before them and the Druids after them, Christians were assumed to engage in incest, infanticide, cannibalism and the worship of a donkey-headed god. Such allegations, fed by misunderstandings of the Eucharist, the fellowship meal and the love of believers for one another, led to dreadful persecutions in the second century, especially at Lyons in what is now France.

Christians were seen a band of atheists because they didn't venerate the Graeco-Roman pantheon, and as immoral conspirators who met in secret to plot Rome's ruin. After all, didn't their founder die a rebel's death on a Roman gibbet? And so in some places they were given a hard time. That there wasn't more widespread persecution was a result of the diverse and in places chaotic state of Roman governance of the Empire. And while Caesars from time to time found the Christians useful scapegoats for political crises or natural disasters, most of them faced more pressing and obvious conspiracies against them. What happened at the eastern end of the Empire, providing it didn't result in armed uprising (as in Judea in AD 66), didn't really matter as much as what was happening on their doorstep in Rome.

22

Making sense of the cross

At Corinth, where debate about the meaning of life centred on the eloquence rather than the substance of the presentation, Paul told the simple story of a crucified man (1 Corinthians 1:18 – 2:5). To his bemused audience, crucifixion was just a gruesome way Rome had of dispatching its enemies. Like electric chairs, gallows and gas chambers, it was not a topic of polite after-dinner conversation or of religious proclamation. Until, that is, the church was born. For the followers of the crucified Jesus, the cross was a symbol of victory, hope, new life and forgiveness. Speaking about it unleashed the power of God in a needy world.

Early Christianity was shaped by the cross. Born in blood on this most cruel of state-inspired killing machines, every element of the Christian story found its meaning in the cross. As they pondered the events of the first Good Friday, the apostles came to see the crucified man standing at the centre of all God's dealings with his world.

The bizarre victory

The New Testament's understanding of the cross is like a jigsaw: all the pieces need to be in place to get the whole picture. But the whole picture is so vast, we can't take it in all at once. So we'll look at the pieces one by one and then see how two New Testament writers fit them together to address their readers' needs.

1. *Victory over God's enemies.* Usually, in a battle, the one left standing at the end is declared the victor. He may be bloodied, but at least he's still alive. The Christians, however, declared that the crucified man, the one bleeding to death under the darkened sky on Good Friday, was the winner. So who was the loser? All the powers ranged against him – from Herod and the temple authorities to Rome, from religious rituals to philosophical systems, from the pagan gods to the devil and all his angels – powers that kept ordinary people in thrall to fear and death, sin and servitude. On the cross, Jesus took them all on and won, emerging victorious in his resurrection on the first Easter Day. The message of the cross is the best news ever.

This theme is particularly central in Paul's writing. Through Jesus' sacrifice, we are set free from sin and death and the religious systems they use to enslave us. And this gives us confidence to know that no enemy can gain the ultimate victory over us (see Romans 8:1–4, 31–39; cf. Galatians 3:13). This is possible because Jesus disarmed the principalities and powers through his cross (Colossians 2:15). The picture is of the triumphant army processing into Rome and leading its vanquished foes so that everyone could see their defeat and ridicule them. This picture of victory through suffering also lies at the heart of John's portrait of Christ in Revelation (especially Revelation 5:5–6).

2. *The end of exile and the dawn of a new age.* The Jews of Jesus' day believed themselves to be still in exile: if not physically, then certainly spiritually. The promises of the prophets concerning the age to come had not yet been fulfilled (e.g. Isaiah 43:1–7; Ezekiel 37:12–14; Hosea 6:1–2). One reason for the continuing exile was that God's enemies still ruled over God's people. On the cross Jesus defeated those enemies, so the homecoming of the people of God could begin.

Peter says times of refreshing (an image of the age to come) will come to those who put their faith in Jesus, who suffered for them (Acts 3:17–21). Paul talks of Christ rescuing us through his cross from this present evil age (Galatians 1:4) and urges his readers to live according to the principles of the age to come, initiated by Jesus, rather than according to this present evil age which is dominated by enslaving philosophies and religions (Colossians 2:8). In Ephesians he talks at length about how, through faith in Jesus' death for us on the cross, we are transferred from this age to the age to come and united in God's household with all those who have faith, regardless of their ethnic, social or religious background (2:1–22). Hebrews too speaks of Christians tasting the life of the age to come through the cross of Jesus (6:1–6).

3. *The payment of a ransom.* Closely linked to the idea of exile is the notion that we are in bondage until we are set free through the cross. Jesus talked of giving his life as a ransom for many (Mark 10:35–45). Paul spoke of believers being redeemed from sin (that is, a price was paid to release them from slavery) through the blood of Christ shed on the cross (Ephesians 1:7; Galatians 3:13). Peter reminds his readers that they were redeemed by the precious blood of Jesus (1 Peter 1:18). And the writer to the Hebrews speaks of Jesus establishing a new covenant of forgiveness through the shedding of his own blood, by which he ransomed us from sin (9:11–14).

All these writers are picking up a theme introduced by Isaiah (43:1–7), where God says that he will ransom his people from exile by giving peoples in exchange for them.

4. *Reconciliation.* This is a key theme in Paul. Through the cross, says the apostle, God will reconcile all things to himself (Colossians 1:19–20; cf. Ephesians 1:10). This is possible because on the cross Jesus defeated all the forces that prevented such a reconciliation taking place. It means that each one of us can be individually reconciled to God as part of his new people (Romans 5:10–11).

Paul particularly applies this theme to the church. In the community of Christians, he says, God is reconciling people who were previously at odds with one another. This is a key theme in Ephesians (2:11–22) and in 2 Corinthians, where Paul is seeking to be reconciled himself to a church that has fallen out with him in a big way. The ground of his hoped-for reconciliation is the cross of Christ and the apostolic ministry of proclaiming that cross to a needy world (2 Corinthians 5:11–21).

5. *Expiation and propitiation.* The cross was fundamentally about dealing with sin. It is human sin and rebellion that cuts us off from God, leads us into exile, gives the rebellious powers freedom to wreak havoc on earth and enables religions and philosophies to enslave us in their distorted systems of belief. This places us under the wrath of God, that is, facing the dire consequences of his judgment of 'guilty' which he hands down to each one of us. Through the cross, however, God smashed the hold that sin has over us and the world.

John applies this very personally in his first letter where he says that each of us needs to recognize and acknowledge that we have sinned against God, before he goes on to assure us that God will forgive us (1:8–10). Why? Because of the cross (2:2). Jesus, says John, is the 'atoning sacrifice' for our sins (the Greek word means 'expiation' or 'propitiation'), and not only for ours, but also for the sins of the world. This is the depth of the Father's love for each of us (cf. 4:10).

The writer to the Hebrews makes this a central theme in his exposition of what God has done through Jesus. He reminds his mainly Jewish readers that forgiveness depends on the shedding of blood (9:22); he talks about the Old Testament sacrificial system as a shadow or forerunner of what God was to do through his Son. And he tells us very clearly that it was on the cross that Jesus dealt with sin once and for all through shedding his own blood (Hebrews 9:1–10:18, especially 10:12–14).

Paul makes this idea the centrepiece of his account of how God is creating one new people out of all the nations of the earth through their faith in Christ. Having outlined the fact that we're all in the same boat because of our sin (Romans 1:18 – 3:20), Paul explains that redemption came through Jesus because God offered him as a 'sacrifice of atonement' (Romans 3:25). In Greek, this term is one word and means 'expiation' or 'propitiation', and is used in the Greek Old Testament to translate the Hebrew for 'mercy seat', that part of the Holy of Holies where the blood of the sacrifice was thrown so that God's wrath would be turned away from his people for another year.

6. *The example of true spirituality.* Jesus lived among us as a servant, one whose life of obedience to God's will was shaped by and lived under the shadow of the cross (Luke 22:24–27). He indicated in no uncertain terms that all who followed him must likewise shoulder the cross and die (Luke 14:27).

This is a key theme taken up by the New Testament writers as they reflected on what the cross meant for our daily lifestyle. For Paul, it meant that he died and Christ lived through him (Galatians 2:20; 6:14); that is to say that he consciously modelled his lifestyle on that of Jesus and looked to the Holy Spirit to help him to live the same way. This was how he exercised ministry. Then as now, many saw religious leadership as a way of wielding power and gaining status. For Paul, it meant sharing the sufferings of Christ (Colossians 1:24–27) and exercising his ministry in the spirit of Jesus (cf. 2 Corinthians 5:11–21). It was the pattern of life that he commended to every believer (Philippians 2:1–11; 3:10–14). Peter too saw Jesus' embrace of the cross as the example that all Christians should follow in the ups and downs of their lives (1 Peter 2:18–25, especially 21–23).

Fleshing out an idea

All New Testament theology was for living. The writers didn't hatch grand-sounding ideas just to look clever and baffle their readers. The point of the teaching was that it is the truth, and the truth sets us free and transforms our lives into the likeness of Christ.

We'll look briefly at two passages shaped by the theology of the cross and see what each writer is saying about the doctrine and its implications for how we should live.

Hebrews 2:9–18

Hebrews is structured around four key Old Testament texts. Chapters 1 and 2 take their cue from Psalm 8, a poem about how human beings are only a little less glorious than God and have been given authority to reign over all creation. But Hebrews is written to Jewish believers who are struggling to keep hold of their faith. They aren't reigning: sin is, and Caesar is.

But, says this writer, we see Jesus (verse 9), the fulfilment of Psalm 8. He is reigning because he suffered death, and through that death routed the enemies of God and his people, the forces that prevent us from reigning in the way foreseen by Psalm 8. These verses force us to look forward to the age to come where creation will be restored, where we will reign, where the exile will finally be over and we will be home at last.

And all this will happen because of the cross. Look at what the author tells us Jesus achieved through the cross: he reigns (verse 9), he is able to bring many sons and daughters to glory (to reign with him) through his suffering (verses 9b–10), he has destroyed the enemies of God who keep us in fearful bondage (verses 14–15) and he made atonement for sin so that we can know God's forgiveness (verse 17 – a theme the author takes up in 9:1 – 10:18).

But even more than this is going on. Jesus, our brother, the one who knows how tough life is, who suffers alongside us, is able to help us if we follow in his footsteps. When we put our faith in him, says the writer to the Hebrews, he calls us brothers and sisters, he leads us from the darkness of exile to the brightness of home, he breaks the power of sin in our lives so that we might share his reign, and he comes alongside us to help us in our time of need, encouraging and strengthening us to remain loyal as he did and so share his glory. And all this is possible, the writer says, because God equipped Jesus to be our Saviour in this way through what he suffered (2:10, 18).

1 Corinthians 1:18 – 2:5

Paul is writing to a church tearing itself apart. In particular, its leaders seem to be more interested in power and status than in following in the footsteps of a suffering Messiah. For them, religion was about eloquence and secret wisdom that gave them a leg up over other people. To them Paul brought afresh the message of the hanged man (Christ crucified).

To those who set such great store by wisdom (by which Paul meant the eloquent rhetoric of the salon philosophers of Corinth's café élites) he pointed out that the message of the cross sounded like foolishness (1:18). But, he went on, such wisdom never freed a single person from bondage, brought them respite from a guilty conscience or gave them a platform to change the world for good.

But the message of the hanged man, Christ crucified, though apparently folly to Gentiles and a stumbling-block to Jews, is the means God has chosen to transform sinners and a fallen creation and usher in the age to come.

The cross, says Paul, is the wisdom of God, for only God was wise enough to hatch a plan that defeated the powers ranged against him by embracing death. It is also the power of God, for through the suffering Messiah God has dealt with sin and death and enabled people to be reconciled to him and to one another. Truly weakness is the way of lasting strength (1:23–25).

But he doesn't leave it there. He goes on to remind his readers that before they met Christ and were moulded into God's new people, they didn't amount to much. For all their supposed eloquence and insight, they were not the movers and shakers of Corinthian society. But that was good, because God has particularly chosen the poor, the power-less, those at the bottom of the heap, to be recipients and messengers of his good news (1:26–28).

When Paul first came to Corinth, he came with the apparently simple message of the crucified Jesus. And he admits he was nervous about it (2:3). After all, in a city that pays attention only to ideas that come with all the fireworks of eloquence and sophistry, the tale of a crucified Jewish carpenter is hardly likely to turn heads. But it did. Because in the telling of the story there is the power of the Holy Spirit to change lives and set people free.

At the heart of the message of the cross – as at the heart of this passage – is Christ, our 'righteousness and sanctifica-tion and redemption' (1:30). 'Righteousness' here almost certainly means 'faithfulness to God's promises'. What Paul is saying is that in the cross God proved his faithfulness to the promise he had originally made to Abraham, that through his family all the nations of the earth would be blessed. Furthermore, in the cross, people were being set apart (made holy) from the present evil age in order that they might enjoy the fruits of the age to come. And in the cross they were bought from slavery into freedom so that as free people they might live to the glory of God in the world.

No wonder Paul had started the letter by saying that this church had been enriched in every way (1:5). The message of the cross releases the power of God into people's live to transform them into the likeness of Christ – even hopeless cases like the first Corinthian believers. Which means there's hope for you and me.

23

A standard to live by

As the second Christian century dawned, all the apostles, the witnesses of Jesus' life and ministry, were dead and gone. Other people who had been involved from the earliest days of the new movement were also dying off. The need was growing for a body of teaching that everyone could trust, a reliable record of what Jesus had said and done and what the apostles had taught about him.

The simplest way of keeping that record was in written form. After all, the church had inherited what we call the Old Testament from the Jews. It made sense, therefore, to put alongside these writings the texts that preserved and communicated the truth about Jesus.

But which writings? By the end of the first century there were probably hundreds of letters, books, sermons, apocalypses and documents of various kinds about Jesus or his followers. Which ones told the truth, the whole truth and nothing but the truth?

Some of the twenty-seven books that make up our New Testament were regarded as special almost from the day they were written. Many of Paul's letters, for instance, were being treated as Scripture even during Paul's lifetime, as Peter observes in his second letter, written before AD 64. He tells his readers that some of what Paul says is difficult to grasp, and that people are inclined to twist what he's saying to suit their purposes, 'as they do the *other* scriptures' (2 Peter 3:16). In other words, Peter is saying, 'Take Paul seriously, because his words are inspired by God.'

It is likely that John's Gospel was very quickly seen to have the mark of truth about it. The other three Gospels also seem to have rapidly established themselves as having a unique authority, despite the fact that many 'lives of Jesus' had been written, as Luke mentions at the beginning of his account.

So, how shall we decide, then?

But what was it that made these books special? Three things seem to have worked together to persuade the leaders of the church in the second and third centuries that the books of our New Testament were uniquely authoritative.

The first mark that people looked for was some connection with an apostle. It was to the twelve apostles that Jesus had entrusted the job of preaching the good news about himself and teaching people all that he had taught. To the Twelve Jesus added Paul, the one he called after his resurrection with the special job of opening up the church to the Gentiles. Writings that were connected with these people were likely to have the ring of truth about them. So it is not surprising that probably by the end of the first century, and certainly by the middle of the second, the thirteen letters that bear Paul's name were being treated as Scripture alongside the Old Testament.

So too were the four Gospels, John's because it was written by the apostle, Matthew's likewise (though that has always been questioned), Mark's because he was associated with Peter, and Luke's because he was a colleague of Paul. Alongside those, 1 Peter and 1 John were very quickly regarded as special, because they were written by apostles, as was the Acts of the Apostles, because it was written by Luke.

The other seven New Testament books – Hebrews, James, 2 Peter, 2 and 3 John, Jude and Revelation – were accepted in some churches but not others. There were problems with them that had to be resolved before they could be accepted by everyone. Hebrews, for instance, was anonymous, so it was very hard to link it with an apostle. There were doubts about 2 Peter and Jude, since they quoted from books that were not in the Old Testament and seemed to be treating them as Scripture. James had not been an apostle and, as the church grew in the Gentile world and shrank in the Jewish world, his association with Jerusalem and Judaism was viewed with a little suspicion.

The second test which was applied to books to see whether they met the mark and could be treated as Scripture was whether they taught the truth or not. Many of the writings circulating in the second and third centuries contained things about Jesus that were right, but they also contained material that ranged from interesting speculation to complete nonsense, and so they were deemed to be unhelpful in teaching the truth. After all, Scripture was meant to be truth that helped people to grow in their understanding of God and salvation. Material that didn't do that couldn't be Scripture. But the seven books about which there were doubts certainly did seem to help people grow as Christians.

Now, that's inspired!

The third test was linked to the second, and it had to do with the effects a particular book or letter had on its readers. Do I feel God speaking to me as I read it? Am I able to base decisions on its teaching? Would I trust my life to these words? Does following this teaching lead to God blessing me and my church? These questions are subjective but important. This third test, linked with the other two, worked to bring together the books that make up our New Testament, because the overwhelming majority of Christians felt that these writings were especially inspired by God, just as the Old Testament was.

It was not until the fourth century that a formal list of the twenty-seven books was drawn up. It is called the canon of the New Testament, 'canon' meaning 'rule' or 'standard'. But all that happened in the fourth century was that the church formally recognized what the Holy Spirit had been telling them for a very long time: 'These books are special. Read them, trust them, live by them.'

Ten books to further your fun with the New Testament

As well as a Bible (The *NIV Study Bible* is a good one) and the complete Crossway Bible Guide series on the New Testament, here are some basic books that anyone wanting to get the best out of the New Testament ought to own or have access to.

Robert Banks, *Paul's Idea of Community* (Hendrickson, second edition, 1994). An excellent introduction to Paul's teaching on the church.

Paul Barnett, *Bethlehem to Patmos* (Hodder and Stoughton, 1989). A helpful overview of the first Christian century.

Craig Blomberg, *Jesus and the Gospels* (Apollos, 1997). A good introduction to all the critical questions about interpreting the Gospels and life of Jesus.

Luke T. Johnson, *The Writings of the New Testament* (SCM, second edition, 1999). An indispensable introduction to every New Testament book; superb on the New Testament's teaching about the resurrection of Jesus.

I. Howard Marshall (ed.), *New Testament Interpretation* (Paternoster, 1979). Recently reissued in a very affordable series, this is a rock-solid introduction to all the critical questions of New Testament interpretation by a top-notch evangelical scholar.

Tom Wright, *The Challenge of Jesus* (SPCK, 2000), and *What Saint Paul Really Said* (Lion, 1997). Incapable of writing an uninteresting sentence, Tom Wright is the most exciting scholar working on the New Testament today. These two books are popular introductions to his more scholarly works. Absolutely indispensable.

Finally, three dictionaries from IVP are worth acquiring. They are expensive, so perhaps a church could buy them for all its home-group leaders and others to have access to:

J. B. Green and S. McKnight (eds.), *Dictionary of Jesus and the Gospels* (IVP, 1992).

R. P. Martin, G. F. Hawthorne and D. G. Reid (eds.), *Dictionary of Paul and his Letters* (IVP, 1993).

R. P. Martin and P. H. Davids (eds.), *Dictionary of the Later New Testament and its Developments* (IVP, 1997).